A History of SPIRITUALISM AND THE OCCULT IN SALEM

A History of SPIRITUALISM AND THE OCCULT IN SALEM

The Rise of Witch City

Maggi Smith-Dalton

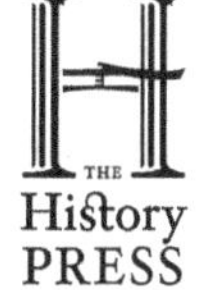
THE History PRESS

Published by The History Press
Charleston, SC 29403
www.historypress.net

First published 2012

Manufactured in the United States

ISBN 978.1.60949.551.0

Library of Congress CIP data applied for.

Notice: The information in this book is true and complete to the best of our knowledge. It is offered without guarantee on the part of the author or The History Press. The author and The History Press disclaim all liability in connection with the use of this book.

For my darling husband, Jim, the light of my heart and soul
and
in loving memory of
beloved friends and family
who have traveled…beyond

Contents

Acknowledgements

There are so many people to thank, and if I have inadvertently neglected someone, I beg their forgiveness (I plead sleep deprivation!). The list of wonderful people who helped me in my journey during the research of this book includes local colleagues Bob Booth, Nelson Dionne and Jerry Curley, who have graced me with their friendship and shared historical interests with me for many years. Special thanks to Joe and Jeanie Galvin for *many* kindnesses—and the gift of friendship. At the Salem Public Library, Jane Walsh shows daily how wonderful a reference librarian can be. The Peabody Essex Museum's Phillips Library is a true gem, and I thank the librarians and staff, including Sidney E. Berger, Kathy Flynn, Irene Axelrod and Andrew French. At the Peabody Essex Museum (PEM), curators Dan Finamore and Karen Kramer Russell generously shared their insights with me about sailors/seafaring and Native American "shape-shifting" culture (and so much more!). I owe very special thanks to my talented friend and colleague at the PEM, April Swieconek, the very definition of a gracious lady. The Peabody Essex Museum, under the inspiring leadership of Dan Monroe and Lynda Hartigan, has given me many hours of delight and intellectual enrichment and is the living continuum, the very heart, of Salem's historically awesome intellectual culture. More friends and colleagues to thank for always making me feel welcome there include Whitney Van Dyke and curator Phillip Prodger.

Thanks also to my friend Neil Gladd and to the staff at the Rare Books Department at the Library of Congress; to Lieutenant Conrad

Prosniewski of the Salem Police Department; and all the helpful scholars from the H-AMSTDY discussion network who helped me track down great resources on Swedenborg. Thanks also to the wonderfully patient and supportive Jeff Saraceno, Dani McGrath and project editor Darcy Mahan at The History Press.

I owe a lifelong debt of gratitude and undying admiration to my Skidmore American Studies mentor, Dr. Gregory M. Pfitzer, an exemplary historian, and to the inspiration and never-failing support of my mentor at Lesley University, Dr. Meenakshi Chhabra.

My husband, Jim Dalton, is the blessing of my life. Though living with a wife who is sometimes more than a bit distracted, and insanely busy himself, he is never-failing in his love, support and understanding.

As always, if you have any questions, feel free to contact me anytime by visiting my personal website, singingstring.org, and dropping me a line.

Introduction

What a long, strange road it's been.

I look at this new child of mine with a sense of bemusement.

As some of you may know, I included a short look at the "psychic past lives" of Salem in my first book, *Stories and Shadows from Salem's Past: Naumkeag Notations*. It was kind of fun stuff, I thought, intriguing, to be sure, but I didn't give it much thought beyond that brief treatment. I thought it might give me another article or two someday, maybe even another book, but I didn't plan to revisit the subject anytime particularly soon.

So, how did I get here?

A Bit of Backstory

In the past two years, my projects included two new recordings of nineteenth-century historical music, immersing me, as usual, in "listening to" the emotional life of the century. I also recently completed and presented scholarly work on the role of music in civic public ritual in post–Civil War and Gilded Age Salem and Boston. As I did all this research thinking about the importance of performance sites and a sense of place in the framing of ritual events and the ways in which these elements operated in a society attempting to recover from the trauma of the Civil War, an article I stumbled across in an issue of the Essex Institute's Historical Collections caught my eye.

It was the published text of a paper read before the institute in 1892 entitled "Were the Salem Witches Guiltless?" Hmmm. I decided I should look into its assertions when my other projects were finished for the summer. In doing so, I confess, I was surprised and hooked. Place, ritual, historical memory…it was all there to explore again.

The story of Spiritualism and the rise of the occult (although, as we will see, they are somewhat separate developments) has a particular twist when surveyed from a Salem, Massachusetts perspective, and this book traces that story.

Salem's journey is our connecting thread here, but my thinking on the matter is broader, more contextual. The rise of Spiritualism and the occult in Salem was one aspect of a rather startling national and international story. A historian, of course, always considers local narratives to be important and essential parts of the puzzle to be assembled, especially when unearthing tales not yet told. Yet caution is wise.

Local historians sometimes fall prey to a myopia that leads the speaker or the writer to extol one's own subject, town, profession or heritage as uniquely virtuous, successful, enterprising or blessed. In the interests of "a good story" (or from longstanding native acquaintance with their subject), the temptation arises for regional authors to attribute motivations to their subjects that cannot always be documented; some even fall into the ultra-literary "omniscient narrator" trap.

Well, although boosterism or hagiography is never appropriate in the toolkit of a modern historian, such intent typically drenches the older historical works one consults for background. The writers of such works were most often those from the dominant regional political, ethnic and/or economic classes. Unsurprisingly, such writers, even the careful ones, were often highly partisan to their class, gender or political beliefs; many wrote with a polemical intent. Memoirs and biographies often display a hagiographic tinge. Most of these writers were amateur historians of predominantly literary bent; the prose style is romantic and often lushly colorful.

Adding to the complications for modern research, New England writers had an overweening tendency to erect and worship at genealogical totem poles; habitual tropes of ancestral adoration must always be expected when reading their works.[1] Salem, where European "founding generation" roots run deep, has been a prime hotspot for this type of veneration.

Ancestral celebration was deemed essential to the construction and maintenance of personal cultural identity for these writers and, they felt, lent authority to their viewpoints. New England played a dominant role in the publication industry in the United States, and thus New England's view of itself and the country assumed a disproportionately influential role in controlling the discourse around historical subjects. New England's leaders were protective of that control. This is especially interesting to observe in the post–Civil War era. Such influence is still detectable to this day.

As we'll see, however, all of this meant that the issue of the 1692 witchcraft trials as a blot on Salem's reputation created continuous cognitive dissonance for those nineteenth-century historians who otherwise wished to boast of the town's illustrious genetic, moral and cultural superiority.

Despite these caveats, local history—even those works that otherwise cannot be relied on for objectivity or disinterested perspective—gives us gems, those small stories that lend natural color and engaging personal detail to the narrative. So this is where professional historical analysis must come into play. Only thus can one maintain balance, perspective and historical integrity.

The past is a foreign country, and we are not native to it. However, we can certainly learn its language, appreciate its landscape and navigate its byways.

The eminent scholar David Blight described the work of the modern historian beautifully during a recent speech about history and memory. He said, in part, "History is what trained historians do. It's a reasoned reconstruction of the past, rooted in research. It tends to be critical and skeptical of human motive and action and it is therefore more secular than what people commonly call 'memory.'"

Blight points out that memory is "owned," treated as "sacred" and "possessed" by a community. Memory centers itself around sites, monuments and place. History, constantly revised, seeks to "understand contexts in all their complexity…and that's why it's harder." History depends on authority bestowed by training and relies on "canons of evidence," while memory carries the "authority of community membership" and "some kind of personal experience." Memory embraces the past emotionally rather than intellectually.

The memory of Salem's "delusion" and the varied responses people had to it were key ingredients in the reception of Spiritualism and the rise of the occult in the nineteenth century, nationwide no less than locally.

That memory of Salem witchcraft, examined historically, is central to our story here.

So, as we look at some key Salem and regional personalities in each chapter as a way of illustrating the larger discussion, keep in mind that this method can only give you an introduction to the complex web in which each of those people operated socially, intellectually and culturally.

The nineteenth century was, to borrow a felicitous phrase, a "very social time," and the communities and groups we'll look at were tightly interwoven not only socially but often professionally. Some of the connections remain "occult" even now. It's my hope this small book will open doors for understanding and give us a good basis for potential future conversations.

SCRYING THE HISTORIAN'S HEART

Where do I stand, personally, on Spiritualism, the role of the occult in Salem or the veracity of occult beliefs?

Well, it is not my task nor is it the intent of this work to address the veracity of those beliefs. That is not the historian's role. I've striven to maintain a balance between objectivity and sympathetic understanding of my subjects. Without both, you cannot approach understanding of what those folks of the past "thought they were up to," (to paraphrase anthropologist Clifford Geertz).

Having lost beloved family members and friends, I understand why the impulse to continue communication with the deceased would prove compelling. I understand why belief in the endurance of one's unique personality, in the progress of one's "self" to greater happiness and continued development beyond material existence could be comforting and reassuring. I understand the depth of the grief that would drive a mother to reconnect with a lost babe, and the idea of my child's continued existence on another plane certainly would provide comfort.

I understand the lure of the mystic, the desire for answers to life's mysteries, a craving for security and just plain curiosity. I can "hear" the emotional life of the times clearly.

Having an enthusiastic layman's acquaintance with the theories of modern physics, I can also readily understand the attraction of "romantic science" for nineteenth-century Spiritualists and their trust in the idea that science had merely revealed truths long intuited by poets, mystics and visionaries. Like the seekers of earlier eras, we too realize we only dimly understand what "reality" is truly made of, and we trust science will bring us increased perspective.

Yet sympathetic understanding must be tempered by objectivity and a healthy skepticism of what was said and examining who said it and why. Balance is key; without it, we cannot hope to add to the body of knowledge, which is the goal of scholarship. We only increase the noise and confusion so evident in our culture otherwise.

REFORM AND THE METAPHYSICAL

My lifelong interest in reform movements, which grew with particular vibrancy in the nineteenth century, was key to my work. Reform movements and the religious expressions with which these eras are so richly endowed so often shared participants, strategies, visions and organization. Spiritualism is an important piece of the nineteenth-century religious and reform mosaic, and I found myself quickly struck by its relevance to broader understanding of historical regional social and political movements.

There is a clear tradition of metaphysical exploration in the historical mosaic of North American cultures. In this assessment, I have valuable scholarly company, far more brilliant than myself, to whom I gladly acknowledge intellectual debt.

I have long held and argued that there has always been a distinctly performative aspect to the American character in every era, in multiple venues. In this evaluation, I also do not stand alone, and one can clearly see this performative aspect in the occult explorations of many of the people we will meet or talk about in this book.

I follow other scholars in treating Spiritualism as a bona fide American religious movement, with reformist and democratic aspirations, and its own structure of internal logic. I agree with the assessment that, although Spiritualism presented a challenge to mainstream religion, which Spiritualists found lacking in relevance to their lives, one of its great attractions (and a key to its rapid growth) was that it could also be adopted alongside and compatibly with one's own individual, more mainstream religious beliefs. In this, Spiritualism presents unique aspects vis-à-vis other contemporary religious movements.

I build on the work of others who have examined Spiritualism as a vehicle for women's empowerment, and an examination of Spiritualism's anarchistic features and its place in a study of American political movements could fill a book of its own.

The rise of Spiritualism and renewed interest in the occult can be understood as part of an evolving and continuing attempt in the nineteenth century to find a satisfactory intellectual and emotional balance between science and religion, between progress and conservatism, between reason and instinct. It can be understood as a reaction to elite authority (dogma and creed) toward democratic populism (the evidence of direct experience).

I was not surprised to find that Spiritualism had its own brand of absolute nuttiness, from those who sought to vociferously defend or decry its philosophies, practices or assertions, to those who—unsurprisingly, in this land of Barnum—saw a golden chance to exploit the vulnerable or the curious in sometimes deplorable ways.

SECRET STORIES AND SALEM'S GLORIES

The pieces I include in this book are selections from a picture far more complex than I expected when I began. After a look at occult incubators earlier in the region's history, we pick up the story in Salem and in America just a bit before the Civil War, and we'll be wrapping up this look at Salem's history just about in time to see the twentieth century dawn.

Much of this era of history in Salem is unexplored, yet is just as fascinating, and certainly just as important, as any other era of Salem's history. The hustle and bustle and incessant motion of Salem's maritime glory days formed vital aspects of Salem's character, to be sure, yet I respectfully contradict those who characterize Salem (then and now) to have fallen on dead and dreary times afterward.

We don't need to run away to sea to find all our adventures in nineteenth-century Salem history.

To quote Johann Wolfgang von Goethe, "Talents are best nurtured in solitude; character is best formed in the stormy billows of the world." In the lives of Salemites of the mid-nineteenth through early twentieth centuries, gemlike talents developed, not quite so ferociously lashed to worldly and commercial success, not quite so filled with bombastic boast or hyperactive physicality.

From the 1840s to the 1900s, Salem was replete with vision, contemplative courage and determination to reach "beyond borders." Her people simply charted their courses by different stars than ship captains of yore.

Nineteenth-century Salemites joined others worldwide in exploring the uncharted seas of the mind. Practical, supposedly materialistic Americans everywhere fell in love with the seductive quest to explore that mysterious interior horizon. Americans sought solace and emotional satisfaction through the spiritual movements of the nineteenth century, but they also sought sophisticated knowledge, intellectual independence and personal power.

For Salem, however, the risks on these interior voyages were considerably greater than for their fellow seekers in nineteenth-century America. Due to the legacy of her "witchcraft delusion," Salem's vessel carried a heavier load than most as she left her carefully protected harbor.

Foretelling a Future

Like the proverbial tiny mustard seed that sends out unexpectedly lush growth, the questions raised by that little item I found at the end of an article have caused this book to rapidly grow far beyond my initial assumptions about the scope of its subject.

Indeed, a larger, more comprehensive and longer study now raps at my door, demanding to be written, demanding its voice be heard. I will be working with this subject and the questions it raised for me for some time to come. (If there was ever a time for some friendly spirit to help out with a little "automatic writing," this is it!)

Perhaps, though, even after all explorations are exhausted, one question will remain forever unanswered, though much addressed: Does "understanding" that the shadows of death loom inescapably give human life its ultimate true meaning?

This surely is as old a struggle in which humans have ever engaged…and continue to engage.

Let's continue that conversation in the future, shall we? Until then, let me introduce you to some of the people I met along the journey so far, and take you with me as we investigate *A History of Spiritualism and the Occult in Salem: The Rise of Witch City*.

Prologue

Do This in Remembr'ance

The gift of reading the future has challenged the veneration of all the ages. Seers and prophets have laid claim to it, and nations have hung trembling on their rapt and awful lips. Could I but lift the veil that hides some scene about to find its enactment amongst us a century,—a year,—a month to come, there would need no aid from rhetoric or illustration to arrest your thoughts. My rudest utterance would sway the soul...I should be hailed as the darling of supernal powers, and straightway lifted with acclaim to a pinnacle of earthly glory.

To most minds...the past has no magic to charm the fancy or enthrall the will...Like the Ancient Mariner, the antiquary must plead with his reluctant listener for a hearing. What has happened in these streets in days gone by may be quite as engaging and every way as momentous as what is like to happen in these streets in time to come,—may be as strange and weird and startling and fantastic, if you will,—may be as grand and worthy and inspiring and heroic as aught that can ever happen in these streets again...

There are, however, a favored few to whom the self-sacrificing and heroic achievements of the past cry aloud for recognition from the grave...

An Address delivered at
Academy Hall, Salem, September 18, 1896,
by Robert S. Rantoul
for the Seventy-fifth Anniversary
of the Founding of the Essex Historical Society
From the Historical Collections of the Essex Institute Vol. XXXII, 1896.

Robert Samuel Rantoul (1832–1922)
Mayor of Salem (1890–1893)

They were there to sort it out, get at the truth of the matter and settle it (hopefully) with dignity and scholarship.

Stormy weather blew through the streets that final leap day of February 1892 while a "large, intelligent" crowd filled Salem's beautiful Academy Hall at the Peabody Museum (boasting a three-hundred-seat "lecture and concert auditorium"). Logs crackled in the hall's fireplace, the fire dancing merrily. As the old-fashioned clock struck eight, a door opened.

A slowly snaking line of distinguished men emerged from the anteroom, taking their chairs one by one, facing their attentive audience solemnly. They were all leaders; men accustomed to vigorous debate in a classroom, from the pulpit, at every ceremonial community occasion. Every one of them had a reputation for probity, maturity and authoritative knowledge. The Essex Institute, under whose auspices they spoke, was one of the most venerable and respected public education organizations in the region. Their collected writings, and those of their colleagues, were counted among the treasures of the era's considerable literary and academic offerings.

"Every individual present had gone to the meeting fully prepared and expecting to hear concise addresses...And they were well rewarded, as each speaker demonstrated that he had made his address the subject of careful study," opined the news criers the next day.

Careful study does not usually set the stage for agitation, yet everyone noted that these great men were strangely "keyed up." This was no ordinary day in Salem.

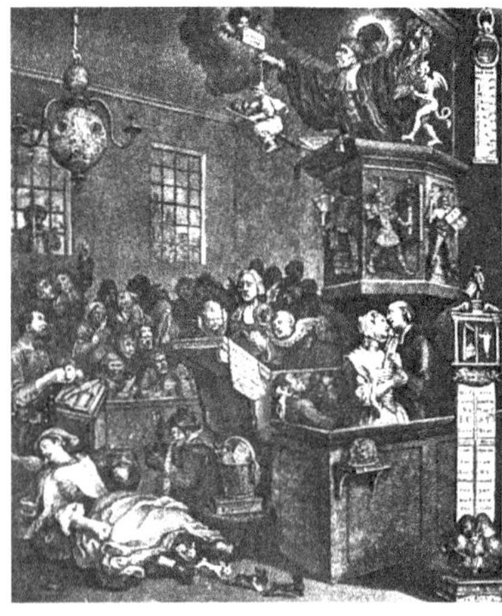

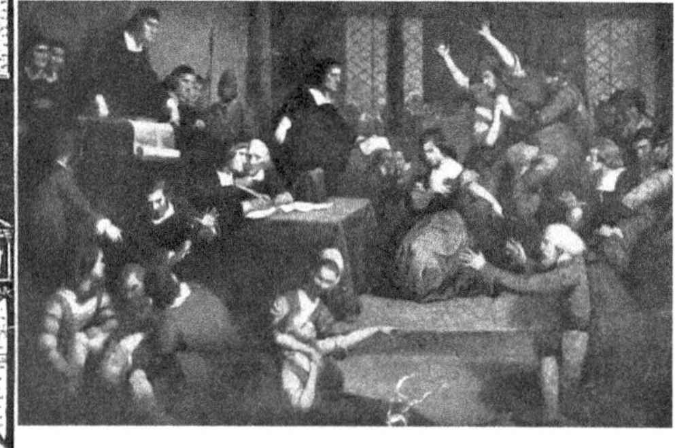

Credulity, Superstition, Fanaticism...*and* Witchcraft.

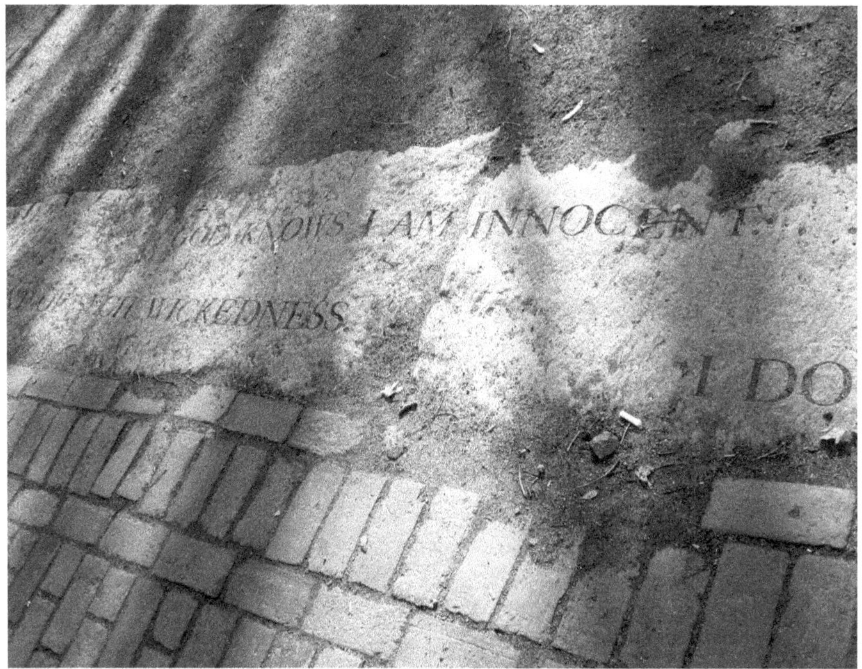

The pleas from the accused still echo around Salem Witch Trials Memorial. Are they heard with respect from visitors to this shrine?

Winfield Scott Nevins (1850–1921), a stalwart citizen and, at forty-two, a respected journalist and writer of town histories, called the meeting to order. He unfolded a document. His most recent research lent his actions that night added authority, having just published a book on the matter before them. Holding the paper up to the light, reading the stern writ aloud, he clearly proclaimed the legal grounds for the arrest of the suspected witch.

Nevins's fellows gazed stolidly at their audience from their places of honor. Just last month, steps had been taken and a committee formed that would place Salem's august Essex Institute, along with Salem itself, prominently on display at the great national exposition to be held in Chicago the following year. The eyes of all people would again be upon the region—and inevitably, those eyes would turn to the haunting heights of Gallows Hill. This evening's 200th anniversary of the witchcraft trials loomed large.

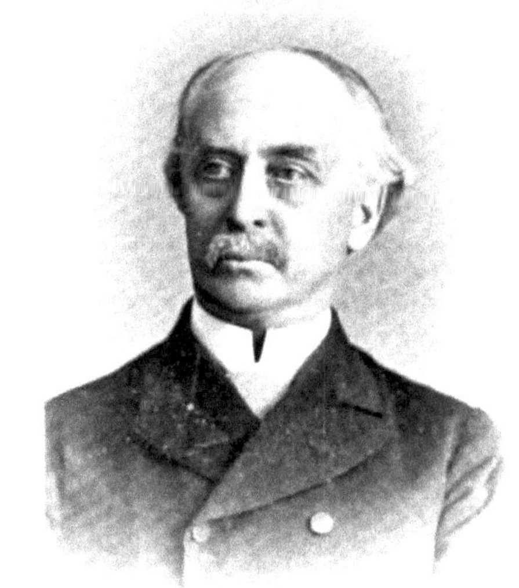

Right: Robert S. Rantoul, circa 1893.

Below: The witch hill broods over Salem—and throws a long shadow.

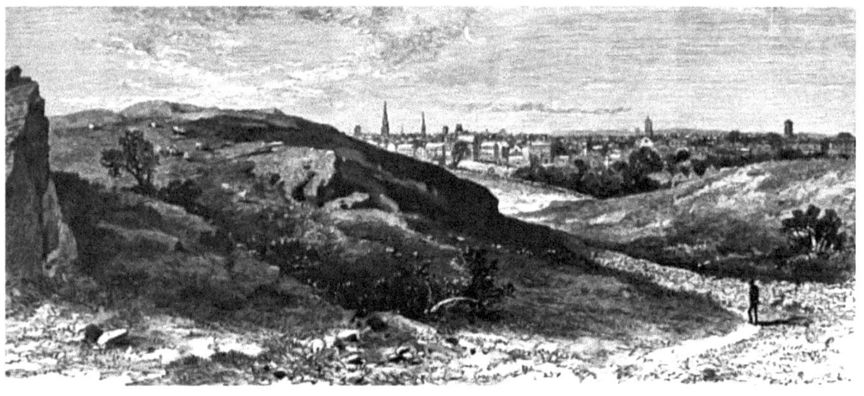

Every one of these men knew about the potential for continuing calumny to be heaped on their beloved town. Duty had brought them here tonight. They felt they held the future reputation of the town in their hands.

Having folded the warrant against one Sarah Good, Nevins remarked briefly that since talk of witchcraft "would go on for ever and ever…it was important that generation after generation should be made to 'understand the correct story.'"

He then turned and introduced Salem's mayor. Handsome and brilliant, an eloquent wordsmith, proud of his heritage and determined to steer Salem to an equally illustrious future, Robert S. Rantoul took the floor.

Outside, the weather worsened.

Dancing flames reddened the walls of the room behind him, and as he readied himself to make opening remarks, he was acutely conscious of the energy flooding the air, uniting the men on the stage in one great impulse.

This was something they would all rather just forget.

Chapter 1

"Old Salem is Gone"

And while the years, an endless host, Come pressing swiftly on,
The brightest names that earth can boast Just glisten, and are gone.[2]

A Portrait of Nineteenth-Century Salem

Salem, Massachusetts, arguably since its founding, was a town devoted to the life of the mind. By the nineteenth century, science, literature, history and the arts were demonstrably important to most Salemites, who were proud of their unique and venerable institutions of learning, their libraries and their famous museum.

Salem wasn't unique in all aspects, of course. Like other old New England towns, it displayed intense preoccupation with its genealogical heritage and harbored an insular, exclusionary group of elites (in fact, visitors sometimes remarked at just how peculiarly and stubbornly insular they seemed to be).

Like other towns across America, Salem also harbored an undercurrent of ethnic and racial prejudice against newcomers. It was the scene of bitter interfaith quarrels, social splits and personality-driven feuds—also just like any other town, but with, perhaps, deeper roots to discord than others.

Founded in 1626, the town's longevity, no less than its cultural advantages, contributed to Salem's ability to send numerous leading citizens to serve on the national and even international stage, the fact of which the town was, truth be told, rather vain.

Salem became the second city in Massachusetts to incorporate (in 1836), dedicating its beautiful new Greek Revival–style city hall on Washington Street in the summer of 1838.

Antebellum Salem settled into quiet channels of economic and cultural endeavor after 1830 or so, which caused some to consider the town "dull" by comparison to earlier eras of global maritime commerce. Yet many (especially the well-to-do, enjoying the financial legacy of the world-trade days) cherished the quiet. The city had enough of an economic "middling" or middle class to ensure that organizations such as the Salem Lyceum would attract large audiences to lectures and concerts.

The average middle-class Salem citizen was keen to learn and to "progress," and, even though Lyceum guidelines urged lecturers to avoid polarizing or controversial subjects, new ideas, however calmly offered, invariably sparked lively debate. Adult education was a keenly sought experience.

Looking back from 1887, Marianne Cabot Devereaux Silsbee (1812–1889) described Salem in mid-century:

> *…they were emphatically good old times; times of respectability, of comfort, of honest toil and elegant leisure, of steady thrift, of modest charities. Moderate times they were, knowing little excess, admitting of no extraordinary action, but so pleasant, so genial, so real, that I would fain describe to the young folks of nowadays the ancestry which gave a certain significance to Salem by the occupations of their industrious, methodical lives, the distinguished characters who made it a noted little place, and the numerous oddities who added piquancy to the daily food of life.*[3]

Due to this long tradition of devotion to education and culture, Salem could continue to claim elevated regional, and even national, cultural status. The East India Marine Society and Peabody Museum of Science lay at the heart of Salem's sense of its identity as a superior, genteel cultural center, as did the venerable Essex Institute, organized in 1848 by the union of the Essex Historical Society and the Essex County Natural History Society.

Salemites were acutely aware and proud of their town's prominent historical identity, yet many expressed deep anxiety over retaining their "special" place in national history. Members of the various intellectual and educational organizations in town felt duty-bound to address that anxiety.

In the introduction to "Cities and Towns," volume one of *The History of Essex County, Massachusetts* (a massive work in which Salem takes a lion's share of space), we read:

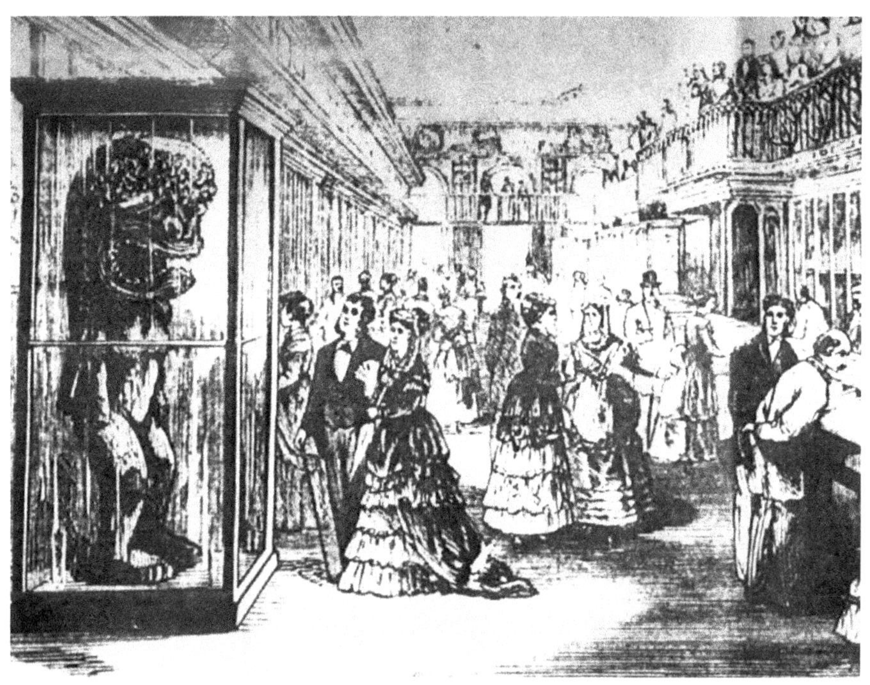

The exotic displays at the Peabody Academy of Science drew large crowds throughout the nineteenth century. This illustration from *Frank Leslie's Illustrated Newspaper,* September 1869, gives us an idea of the atmosphere.

> *The old Salem is gone. The men, the commerce, the Puritan spirit, the high-bred courtesy, the stately ways, the great men and women with strong local attachments,—these are gone. Nothing remains of the most stirring epoch in the life of the town but names, places, and a decreasing number of families who trace their ancestry back of the nineteenth century, in Salem.*
>
> *A new Salem has taken place of the old. A city stands where the old town won its renown,—a city with railroads, horse-cars, electric lights and cotton-mills, and a large foreign population. The mansions built by merchants of English descent and training are inhabited by operatives in the mills or laborers, who have no interest in the old ways or the former inhabitants. The Irish brogue and the French language are heard now where pure English was once the rule…*

The writer goes on to opine about the "new" Salem arising from the ashes of the old:

> *The ideals of character which were the Puritan's finest contribution to the resources of modern civilization, honored and revered on the spot which gave them birth, will be constant sources of virtue and intelligence…*
>
> *The Athenaeum, the Essex Institute, the Peabody Academy of Science and the societies and individuals that are attending to music and art are yet to be heard from in a way not unworthy of Salem. The idea is being cultivated that wealth is not the sole foundation of a good society…Now attention is turned to the other things which are seen to be permanent and of staple value in good society. The new Salem will be rich, but its cultivation will not be incidental. It will be held to be or primary importance, and with religion, good morals and wisdom, will enrich the national life far beyond any material contributions…*[4]

Culture, Music and the Arts: Salem's Well-Tended Garden

In 1799, Salem captains and mariners who had sailed beyond the Cape of Good Hope or Cape Horn formed a new (and quite exclusive) East India Marine Society.

One of their goals was to establish a "cabinet of natural and artificial curiosities," so, as a famous toast made in 1804 trumpeted, "that every mariner may possess the history of the world."

In a frequently cited 1995 *New England Quarterly* article, James M. Lindgren sketched the unforgettable scene of the museum's dedication:

> *A vast concourse of citizens…lined the streets of Salem…on 14 October 1825 to watch a procession held by the shipmasters of the East India Marine Society…Winding its way past brightly decorated buildings, the cavalcade was preceded by an elaborate palanquin in which sat a Salemite dressed out as an Indian prince. Other mariners and merchants in Asian attire carried trade goods from the Orient or curiosities for the museum.*[5]

The prideful procession was followed by a lavish banquet, at which President John Quincy Adams, Boston's second mayor Josiah Quincy and Justice Joseph Story went round and round with the others through forty-four toasts (the president wisely—or exhaustedly—quit after the twentieth) accompanied by music, fanfare and boozy self-congratulation on the importance of Salem's "Trade to India," to the Orient and the wealth trade had brought to city and country alike. Society members paraded annually for several years to show off new acquisitions.

Thus, in the center of town, a permanent reminder of Salem's global connection was established. By the early 1830s, the Salem East India Marine Museum held "the largest collection of Oriental artifacts in the country."[6] Familiarity with Oriental motifs, exotic scents and scenes played a large part in the interior life and imagination of Salem citizens (some of whom became prominent scholars of the arts and culture of Oriental nations). This, perhaps, has not been fully appreciated for its role in the growth of Salem's occult and metaphysical beliefs.

In his study of how the Salem museum may have influenced the work of Nathaniel Hawthorne, George Washington University professor Jee Yoon Lee observed, "The museum…created a narrative of Salem's worldliness…The museum items…worked together to display how Salem perceived foreignness."[7]

The artifacts in Salem's great museum, "the early nineteenth-century mythic and mystical objects from the East that Salem exhibited," juxtaposed in a setting foreign to their origin, offered an opportunity for visitors to construct narratives about themselves and about who "they" (the original creators of the objects) were.

The museum's artifacts nurtured an atmosphere of mystery in which occult fantasies could thrive. Such fantasies, paradoxically, reinforced the town's own sense of anchored American identity. Yet the artifacts in Salem's famous museum undeniably carried the aura of ritual and occult knowledge. For example, Lee tells us, in 1850, a captain sent his artifact accompanied by a descriptive note: "The Chinese god of wealth, having a golden wedge in his left hand and the right hand raised to bless his worshippers. This one I herewith send has been worshipped for about 20 years. I could have procured a new one, but send one that had been worshipped purposely to the East India Marine Museum, Salem, Mass—with Complts."[8] Donations of this type commonly arrived with similar descriptions, serving to underline foreignness of the peoples represented by the artifact.

Demarcations between "us" and "the other" were sharply drawn and observed in all kinds of ways. In 1833, "people of Colour" were excluded from visiting the East India Marine Society museum during its "usual hours of admission," unless they were "attending" other visitors. Women were nervously shepherded by custodians as they gazed upon displays of artifacts and depictions of "primitive peoples" in their sometimes "scanty" garb.

Writing about antebellum Salem, Samuel Roberts Wells commented:

> *There was then an exclusiveness about the place as evident to strangers, and as dear to natives, as the rivalship between Philadelphia and Baltimore.... In Salem society there was a singular combination of the precision and scrupulousness of Puritan manners and habits of thought with the pride of a cultivated and traveled community, boasting acquaintance with people of all known faiths, and familiarity with all known ways of living and thinking, while adhering to the customs, and even the prejudices, of their fathers. While relating theological conversations held with liberal Buddhists or lax Mohammedans, your host would whip his horse, to get home at full speed by sunset on a Saturday, that the groom's Sabbath might not be encroached on for five minutes. The houses were hung with odd Chinese copies of English engravings, and furnished with a variety of pretty and useful articles from China, never seen elsewhere, because none but American traders had then achieved any commerce with that country but in tea, nankeen, and silk.*[9]

In 1937, Caroline Howard King's delightful memoir about her childhood, *When I Lived in Salem*, was published posthumously with a preface from her fellow "literate, talented, austerely sophisticated"[10] friend, socialite Louisa L. Dresel. Born in 1822, "Kiddy" King lived in Salem until 1866; after three decades in Boston, she returned to live the rest of her life on exclusive Chestnut Street. In 1907, just before she died, she completed most of her memoirs. King remembered with affection the effect the East India Marine Society museum's mysterious and occult atmosphere had on her as she was growing up:

> *As far back as I can remember the museum had a mysterious attraction for me. And indeed it was an experience for an imaginative child, to step from the prosaic streets of a New England town, into that atmosphere redolent with perfumes from the East, Warm and fragrant and silent, with a touch of the dear old Arabian Nights about it. From the moment I set my foot in that beautiful old hall, and greeted and was greeted by the solemn group of Orientals, who, draped in Eastern stuffs and camel's hair shawls stood opposite the entrance, until the hour of closing, came, and Captain Saul went through his never-failing ceremony of presenting me with a slip of sandal wood cut from a huge log that stood near the door or a sweet-smelling Tonquin Bean, the hours were full of enchantment, and I think I came as near fairy-land as one ever can in this work-a-day world.... There was an Eastern flavor in Salem then...*[11]

Institutional Intellectualism

Moving on from the museum to survey the rest of the landscape, one finds a staggering list of societies and organizations supporting cultural and intellectual life in nineteenth-century Salem.

The Essex Historical Society

In 1820, Salem mourned the loss of the irreplaceable Reverend William Bentley, one of Salem's most brilliant, prolific and erudite citizens. In view of Bentley's lifelong dedication to Salem, its leaders confidently expected to receive, as almost a birthright, the fruits of the pastor's "accumulation of forty years of local and historical research, during the very period of our most brilliant commercial fame." What could be more natural than to expect to keep this treasure trove of materials within Salem and Essex County's control?

Bentley's will shocked them. His entire legacy was bestowed on others. A large portion of Bentley's library had gone to Allegheny College, in Meadville, Pennsylvania, and most of the rest to the Antiquarian Society in Worcester. Indignation!

The following spring, still reeling from this disappointment, determined that the history of Essex County would, in the future, be preserved locally, some thirty men met at the Athenaeum to plot and plan for a historical society, which they founded officially on June 11, 1821. The yearly meeting was held on the date identified as the anniversary of John Endicott's landing, thus rooting society ritual observance in its Puritan heritage.[12]

Scholars and writers were given honorary membership in what was, from the beginning, an elitist organization. Members zealously collected local Indian relics; solicited town and parish histories, court records, baptismal, marriage and death records; kept journals; and recorded or facilitated commentary on contemporary happenings (much as Bentley, the diarist par excellence, had done).

Genealogies were assembled despite the warnings in Holy Writ that such compilations were akin to "foolish questionings and endless fables and contentions and litigation." Portraits were sought of ancestors, members and other "honored" personages, and familial artifacts were collected.

Authors and publishers deposited their first editions with the grateful society; a comprehensive library of newspapers and other publications was built.

In short, the society was driven to be acquisitive of the past. Annually, ritually, through oratory, lectures and public ceremony, they also instituted a tradition of erudition and gentility and fostered a veneration of ancestry. That veneration in turn nurtured a sense of obligation in younger generations to value continuity, of enduring debt to the past.

The Essex County Natural History Society

September 18, 1828, was a beautiful autumn day. All was deemed perfect for the Essex Historical Society's "magnificent, second-century celebration of the landing of Endecott." A procession flowed from Washington Square and threaded through Samuel McIntire's "fine old archway of the western gate, with its eagle and Washington medallion." The day was filled with pomp, pageantry and, of course, music, and it culminated with a stirring ovation by Justice Joseph Story.

In this teeming, cheering and emotionally charged crowd was a delighted teenager who would prove instrumental to the development of another of the most important intellectual institutions of nineteenth-century Salem and Essex County.

In 1832, that young man, Henry Wheatland (1812–1893), graduated from Harvard College, earning his MD in 1837. Yet he preferred other fields to the practice of medicine. From childhood, he was fascinated by the study of natural history. On voyages to Europe and South America, he collected specimens that later took their place in the cabinets of Salem's museum.

With other young friends, Wheatland organized a "new society for the pursuit of natural science," which "through its system of field-meetings, of lectures, and of fruit and flower shows made its way promptly to general regard."

The Essex County Natural History Society, founded in 1833, became known for its exhibits and attention to matters of horticulture and natural science, the former being a common interest in what was, until the later nineteenth century, still a region predominantly verdant and agricultural in nature.

Salem's record in the science of horticulture was sterling, boasting the nation's foremost pomologist in its ranks: handsome Robert Manning Sr. (1784–1842), better known today as the uncle and guardian of Nathaniel Hawthorne.

This was the great age for science. New England, in particular, was acknowledged as an ideal greenhouse for scientific cultivation, and European journals wrote of the support for science in America with admiration (and more than a tinge of envy).

This deep respect for and energetic activity in the field of science created an atmosphere in which those who later sought scientific proof for spirit communication or had interest in mesmerism and magnetic healing might naturally feel comfortable in pursuing such explorations.

The Essex Institute was organized in 1848, formed by the union of the Essex Historical Society and the Essex County Natural History Society. The two organizations, thus combined, moved their libraries and collections to Plummer Hall. Scientific exhibits and collections were placed across the street at East India Marine Hall, under the care of the Peabody Academy of Science. The academy, supported by a $140,000 bequest from George Peabody in 1867 to support "science and useful knowledge in Essex County," purchased the property and finished the new hall in 1869. The Peabody Museum was dedicated that year at the first meeting of the American Association for the Advancement of Science, another Salem contribution to the larger United States culture.

The institute sponsored and organized lectures, concerts and commemorative events celebrating various historical anniversaries (all accompanied by orations, music and, quite often, feasts and balls).[13]

Despite constant appeals in most bulletins and communiqués to the public for financial support, which increased in urgency throughout the second half of the century, and perennial lamentations that the current generations did not value high culture as they should, it continued to anchor the intellectual life of Salem well into the twentieth century.

The Salem Athenaeum, incorporated in 1810, featured a library built from even older collections (of the Social and Philosophical Libraries). Plummer Hall, built on land bought with a bequest by Caroline Plummer (1789–1854) became the home of the Athenaeum and its library in 1857. Formerly, this site had boasted the boyhood home of prominent historian William Hickling Prescott (1796–1859).

The Salem Lyceum, founded in January 1830 "for the purpose of mutual instruction and rational entertainment by means of lectures, &c," built its permanent home in 1831 at Lyceum Hall. The Lyceum movement was one of the most potent examples of democratic educational opportunities our country has produced. By 1834, there were over three thousand Lyceums in America. Salem had one of the most prominent and respected of the numerous Lyceums in Massachusetts, which, in turn, had more than any other state.

The Salem Lyceum hosted not only orations and concerts, educational programs and lectures, but also scientific exhibits and demonstrations of all types. Salem, in particular, provided a platform for speakers and events of nationwide, and even worldwide, importance. Lyceums would be crucially important to spreading the message of Spiritualism.

Until the latter half of the century (the Lyceum building was torn down in the 1880s), the Salem Lyceum counted heavily in any consideration of the town's nineteenth-century character and historical legacy.

Artistic and Literary Salem

Artistic and literary Salem thrived. Quite beyond the fame of Nathaniel Hawthorne, nearly every Salemite one investigates with any social role, women as well as men, published books, speeches and poetry. Artists and scholars of art born or active in Salem achieved national renown. To name a few: Charles Osgood (1809–1890), who painted, among other things, a well-known portrait of a young Nathaniel Hawthorne; George Southward (1804–1876); sculptor and poet William Wetmore Story (1819–1895); John Rogers (1829–1904), prolific sculptor of "small character groups," a genre in which he dominated; and Ernest Francisco Fenollosa (1853–1908), American Orientalist and educator, later head of the Boston Museum of Fine Arts Oriental department and Columbia University professor.

In regional and national context, this is, of course, an era of remarkable literary flowering; thus Salem's garden bloomed as one prolific plot in a remarkably verdant artistic American landscape.

Musical and Theatrical Salem

Salem Gazette editor Caleb Foote's son Arthur Foote, who would become the first American-born, American-trained composer to receive a master's degree in music (from Harvard) and who enjoyed a long and illustrious career as a composer, teacher and musician in nineteenth- and early twentieth-century Boston, wrote in a 1937 issue of the *Musical Quarterly*:

> *The town of Salem, Massachusetts, where I was born, March 5, 1853, was a quiet, prosperous, self-contained place, not dependent for music and theatre on Boston. It had tradition and cultivation; life there was simple and easy, and is a pleasant thing to look back upon in these restless, anxious days. Salem had a picturesque and stirring history, the rotting wharves being reminders of its vanished merchant shipping, and of the privateers of 1812.*

Later, in his autobiography, he elaborated:

> *Salem was then a city of about 20,000, a very good class of Irish being the only addition to the old inhabitants of English descent...We had one series of first-rate lectures and another consisting partly of lectures and partly of good concerts. We had a life of our own, and were not dependent upon Boston.*[14]

The history of musical and theatrical Salem truly is an impressive story to tell. Salem was simply full of music and was supportive of other performing arts. Even in a time when most music-making was participatory and ubiquitous, and even when considered in a national context, Salem's musical culture was uncommonly serious in intent and unusually rich in talent.

Professional theatrical performances have been documented in town as early as 1769. Theatrical offerings—and early theater invariably included music—were presented again in Salem from the late 1790s through 1830, mostly by professional traveling troupes and solo performers. Most of the presentations were mainstream popular fare imported from England, as was true of the repertoire of all American theaters (strung sparsely up and down the Eastern coast). Salem even continued to enjoy theater during bans on theatrical entertainment in Boston. Amateur performances by schoolchildren and other kinds of performing arts also enlivened the scene.[15]

Live theatrical and musical activity (amateur and professional, including vaudeville) continued throughout the century and was especially vigorous, prolific and influential in the latter half of the nineteenth and early twentieth centuries.

Music was taught in the schools, particularly between 1868 and 1877, and Salem hosted or nurtured well-known musically progressive educators. The city had numerous short- and long-lived musical societies and choral groups; some of these musical groups garnered regional fame. Throughout the nineteenth century, private musical gatherings, mostly organized by women, were a mainstay of Salem's social life. Music stores or bookstores that carried music advertised widely in every era of the city's existence, and music libraries existed within museum organizations and historical societies.

Bands and band music were important components of political, public, social and military ceremonies, and band concerts were frequent and well attended. Even a casual survey of the newspapers of Salem underscores the frequency and popularity of these and other concerts.

The popularity of extravaganzas, circuses, tableaux and theatrics of all kinds provided an extremely receptive community for the spiritualist stage shows and spectacles of the later nineteenth century.

Religious Life

It is in the diversity of Salem's nineteenth-century religious life that we find truly fertile ground for the growth of Spiritualism. The culture allowed for, and indeed fostered, vociferous debate on religious matters and the variety of religious choices that split, turned and peeled off from established Protestant denominations. Groups organized under new or modified belief structures also allowed for the growth of other, more esoteric spiritual searches.

Of course, Christianity itself provided a basis for belief in supernatural beings, influence and manifestations. The arguments for or against Spiritualism were usually couched in the familiar cadence of contemporaneous Protestant Christian discourse.

Churches abounded in nineteenth-century Salem, and many had very deep roots. The First Congregational Society of Salem, founded in 1629, was the first Protestant church organized in America.

Baptists formed a society in 1806; Roman Catholics were able to worship in Salem as early as 1806, and a parish was organized in 1811. St. Mary's Church was erected in 1821. Methodist, Mormon, Universalist, Episcopal, Second Adventist and spiritualist churches all took root in Salem through the second half of the nineteenth century. Churches were also established for black Salemites. The St. Joseph's French Catholic Society for French-speaking immigrants was formed in 1874.[16] The First Church of Christ, Scientist, found a permanent home on Lynde Street by 1908, lasting for much of the rest of that century.[17]

The Society of Friends (Quakers) had survived and triumphed over the history of their persecution in Salem, building a meetinghouse in 1688 on Essex Street; by 1879, they were worshiping freely in a brick church on Pine Street.

Acceptance of and pride in Salem's Quakers (who honored both male and female as having the right to conduct inspired ministry and preaching) were often pointed to as examples of the progress nineteenth-century Salem had made toward religious tolerance since colonial times.

Ethnic Diversity

After the Civil War, the United States experienced a burst of immigration that would crest in the early 1880s; immigrants came from southern and eastern Europe, and later, at the turn of the twentieth century, Jewish immigration (particularly from Russia) increased from rivulet to stream. The Irish continued to emigrate from their sea-tossed island shores. While many immigrants stayed in New York City or headed for the industrial centers of Chicago, New England industries actively cultivated immigrants from French Canada. The result was rapid change in demographics for many cities, including Salem.

In Salem and in the region as a whole, French-Canadians became a highly visible and numerically important group. According to an article in volume 8, number 1 of the Franco-American Institute of Salem's newsletter *La Revue de Salem* (2006), Salem's Franco-American community began in 1856 with the emigration of Pierre Caisse, born in 1815, from Canada to New England.

Polish immigrants began arriving in the United States after 1830, and those who came to Salem tended to settle in the Derby Wharf area, which, after 1910, was home to the House of the Seven Gables settlement house.

By 1900, immigrants from French Canada, Poland and Ireland made up the largest portion of the industrial workforce in town. French Canadians largely settled in the "Point" section of Salem, originally called "Stage Point" and historically a center of coastal economic activity.

Thousands of these immigrant workers were employed in Salem's Naumkeag Steam Cotton Company (Pequot Mills), founded in 1839.

Industry

Salem's industries by 1888 included leather manufacturing and the manufacture of cotton cloth (with the entire business invested in one company: the aforementioned Naumkeag Steam Cotton Company). Other industries included shoe manufacturing; jute-bagging mills; whale oil, white lead, paint, typewriter and car manufacturing. Salem also figures prominently in early adoption of electric lighting.

The Boston and Maine Railroad opened in 1878, and Salem was also connected to the Boston and Lowell Railroad; this greatly aided Salem's commercial growth. In 1874, the Boston, Revere Beach and Lynn Railroad increased summer tourism to the area.

Railroads ruled the era. In 1868, George Pullman incorporated the Pullman Palace Car Company; the first transcontinental railroad in the United States was completed at Promontory Point, joining East and West. Locally, the first railroad tunnel through the Hoosac range in northwestern Massachusetts allowed the Boston and Maine Railroad to connect New Englanders and New York City with unprecedented ease. The Eastern Railroad was chartered in 1836.

The story of the railroad in Salem is multilayered and exceedingly important to the city it became in the nineteenth century. Lecturers of all kinds, including those spreading the ideas of Spiritualism, took advantage of the relative ease of transport to all corners of the country.

Social Attitudes

Prejudice against ethnic minorities, as previously noted, was certainly present in Salem. By 1854, the city and region were active in the nativist American Party, or Know-Nothings—albeit relatively briefly. Stephen Palfrey Webb (1804–1879), twice mayor of Salem (1842–45 and 1860–62), had, between his elections in Salem, moved to San Francisco. He served as mayor there too, winning election with the strong support of the Nativist Party.

Just as anti-immigrant, nativist and social Darwinist sentiments began to build nationwide during the late nineteenth century, so, too, did they increase in Salem.

One notices the absence of immigrants or newcomers, especially those who did not speak English, in the various "official" accountings of Salem life published during the period. The face Salem wished to present to the world was white, Protestant and "venerable."

From the pen of the erstwhile Reverend George Batchelor (1836–1923) comes this example of a contemporaneous "Teutonic germ theory" school of historical thought as he describes the settling of New England in his "Introductory" chapter to *The History of Essex County*:

> *Then New England begins to emerge slowly from the vast, unsurveyed bulk of the continent, and to attract the attention of those in whose keeping were the seeds which, for a hundred generations of English and Germanic life, had been preparing to grow into the social, civil and religious institutions of New England. "God sifted a whole nation," said Stoughton, "That he might send choice grain out into the wilderness." He might have said that the civil and religious institutions of the Germanic race were sifted to furnish precedents, aptitudes and the specific religious impulses out of which to produce the Puritan Church and the New England Commonwealth.*[18]

Lest we think this attitude is confined to this Unitarian minister, throughout two main local histories as well as in the smaller pamphlets, addresses and speeches, the "pure" (superior) New England character is often contrasted with the invasive (and inferior) immigrant, sometimes subtly, ofttimes not.

This excerpt from *The Ships and Sailors of Old Salem; the Record of a Brilliant Era of American Achievement* (1912) by Ralph Delahaye Paine (1871–1925) is also typical of the era:

> *Salem is proud of its past, but mightily interested in its present... But as has happened to many other New England cities of the purest American pedigree, a flood of immigration from Europe and Canada has swept into Salem to swarm in its mills and factories. Along the harbor front the fine old square mansions from which the lords of the shipping gazed down at their teeming wharves are tenanted by toilers of many alien nations...*[19]

Note the use of phrases like "alien" and "swarm[s]," "flood[ing]" a city of "purest American pedigree."

If "Old Salem is Gone," What's Left?

Women are barely mentioned in the Salem section of 1888's *History of Essex County*, save as beloved wives or simply named as daughters. The Salem portion of the *History* occupies nearly 250 pages; in the section devoted to literature, fully three-and-a-half columns are devoted to a panegyric discussion of Nathaniel Hawthorne's life and work. Two columns, in contrast, suffice to account for a dozen or so women writers; one separate column is devoted to Elizabeth Palmer Peabody (1804–1894) and includes her two sisters.

Of course, women were exceedingly active in nearly every aspect of the town's life, public and private: as artists, musicians, actors, organizers, retailers, philanthropists, orators, teachers and, of course, as industrial workers. Salem was also no stranger to activist women.

One interesting manifestation of social challenge can be seen in the ongoing published reactions to a speech given in January 1870 by Mary Ashton Rice Livermore (1820–1905), advocating "The Reasons Why" women should be given the vote and greater equality in every area of life.

During the Civil War, Livermore worked with the Sanitary Commission in Chicago. The U.S. Sanitary Commission was an organization that provided medical care to Union troops in areas where the government could not. After the war, she worked tirelessly for women's organizations such as the American Woman Suffrage Association (serving as president from 1875 to 1878) and the Woman's Christian Temperance Union, wrote for reform periodicals and made speeches nationwide on a variety of reform and liberal causes. In her Salem speech, she stated, "Women who are true women, dislike and are ill-contented with that condition by which they lie back doing nothing and are supported in idleness. If you think we are content to lie back while you are fighting the battles of life, you are mistaken…It is no struggle for vulgar supremacy that we are engaged in. We ask only for equality."[20]

This touched off a virtual firestorm of articles and letters to the editor published over the next few months in the *Gazette*, many of them running angrily or scornfully against women's desires for equality or mocking specific points of Livermore's speech, although a smaller number of reader responses were highly supportive of her main themes.

Livermore, like other progressive women of her era, would turn to Spiritualism late in her life and believed she had been able to contact her husband, Daniel, after his death. In one of her books, she even joked about being taken for a trance medium by strangers. A woman accustomed to speaking out and speaking up, she was well known to Salem audiences.

Women's Clubs and Civic Engagement

Two days before Independence Day, on July 2, 1891, author, activist and inveterate organizer Kate Tannatt Woods, "an officer in the General Federation of Women's Clubs and a member of the New England Woman's Club," opened the door of her house to greet seven guests. The group included Mrs. Grace Atkinson Oliver, a member of the Boston Woman's Club. The lively gathering of ladies meeting in Woods's home that afternoon planned to form yet another of Salem's numerous public associations. At a second meeting later that month, the fledgling club boasted thirty attendees.

With the adoption of a constitution and the founding of the new association (Woods suggesting the name "Thought and Work Club"), Salem made a significant contribution to one of the great social movements of the nineteenth century. Women's clubs were the driving force in so many of the era's cultural, political and charitable achievements and organizations that their importance to the development of the modern United States can hardly be exaggerated.

Kate Tannatt Woods (1836–1910), who was elected president, and Grace A. Oliver (1844–1899), elected vice-president, were, as indicated, well versed in the ways and methods of club organization. Corresponding secretary Ellen A. Brown, recording secretary Abbie L. Read, treasurer Emma S. Almy, auditor Sarah Davis and five more directors filled out the rest of the early Thought and Work Club's official governing group, according to Jane Cunningham Croly's *The History of the Woman's Club Movement in America*, published in 1898.

The aims of the association were broad, yet meshed with the goals of the larger contemporary nationwide movements. Croly (1829–1901) wrote: "The club was established on much the same lines as the New England Woman's Club in Boston, with points taken from various other organizations and some methods of its own. It was the object to make it broad in its work and liberal in its aims."

Since the president and vice-president were published authors, it comes as no surprise that the club did much "good literary work." But, added Croly, the club was also "active in civic affairs. It has labored to improve the schoolrooms, to cleanse the street-cars, and elect women upon the school boards. It has won a half holiday for the clerks in the stores, and presented to the schools a number of fine pictures. It has brought many famous men and women to the old town, and established a headquarters in one of the historic houses, where classes are held and the committee work done."

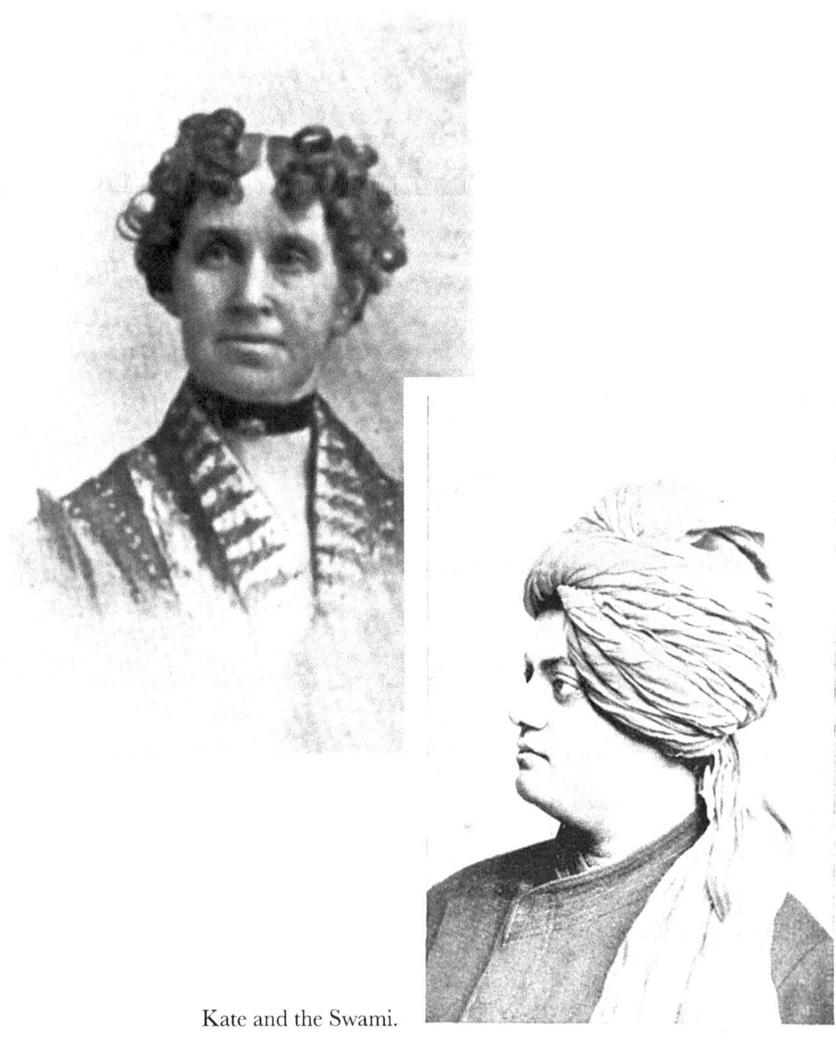

Kate and the Swami.

The Thought and Work Club produced literary publications and established a "book review class." It also sponsored language classes and a civics class, which was "addressed by prominent city officials and State senators." Thus, through all these endeavors, the club assumed an active role in the local community, and since its organizers were also active in larger spheres (for instance, Woods was a founder of the Massachusetts State Federation of Women's Clubs), Salem's women also enjoyed influence beyond city borders. Eventually, the group expanded to more than three hundred members.

Meeting twice monthly, the Thought and Work Club had, by 1898, committees for art and literature, history, education and "home improvement." In 1893, Kate Woods hosted a visiting Hindu, Swami Vivekananda (1863–1902). Woods even gave a garden party for local children with the swami as guest of honor, during which he addressed their curiosity about the lives of children in India.

"How honored by fate you must feel to have been allowed to be of service to this Great Soul. I believe him to be a re-incarnation of some great Spirit—perhaps Buddha, perhaps Christ. He is so simple—so sincere, so pure, so unselfish," wrote journalist and poet Ella Wheeler Wilcox (1850–1919) to Woods in May 1895.

Vivekananda was to speak before the Parliament of Religions conference in Chicago but apparently created a bit of controversy in Salem before he traveled West.

> *...Vivekananda was asked to speak to various groups by his hosts. He took no time to dispel the myth that Hindu religion was a barbaric one, as Christian missionaries had painted such a picture of the religion in the west. This was not well received by local ministries and Vivekananda felt some hostility in their attitudes and manner of questions.*[21]

He gave talks in several of the local churches (sometimes well attended, sometimes not) and was "closely questioned" by ministers at some of them. The swami, generally credited with introducing yoga and meditation practices to Americans, articulated his vision of "universal religion"—one eternal religion superseding sect or creed. Rather predictably, this created much of the controversy he sparked among traditional mainstream religions.

For Spiritualists, who famously adhered to no creed and no specific theology, his message would have seemed welcome and even commonplace.

Pulling Back to Look at the Larger Picture

The period from 1868 to 1889 was an era in which the modern United States was forged. The largest part of this era takes its moniker "The Gilded Age" from a book by Mark Twain and Charles Dudley Warner and is usually characterized by discussions of political corruption, greed and financial manipulations and huge accumulations of wealth by businessmen leading to a marked state of economic inequality and the sharpening of class lines.

Traditional authority and genteel character were being questioned on nearly every front. A sense of personal identity was also under negotiation for those seeking a "place in the sun," and the tenor of the times framed that negotiation, most often, in terms of material gain.

The Western United States loomed large in the imagination. Salemites, like other Americans, went West with some regularity, mostly in pursuit of economic opportunity, and many never returned. Some, like Salem's Mormons, went West to stay for religious reasons. Spiritualists are mentioned as spreading their beliefs westward in a number of sources; an unnamed Salemite was referred to as proselytizing in Hannibal, Missouri, in *Modern American Spiritualism* by Emma Hardinge [Britten](1823–1899), a historian of the first two decades of the religion.

The 1848 Gold Rush began the same year that the Fox sisters began to communicate with spirits in Hydesville, New York; that same year saw the first Women's Rights Convention at Seneca Falls, not all that far from

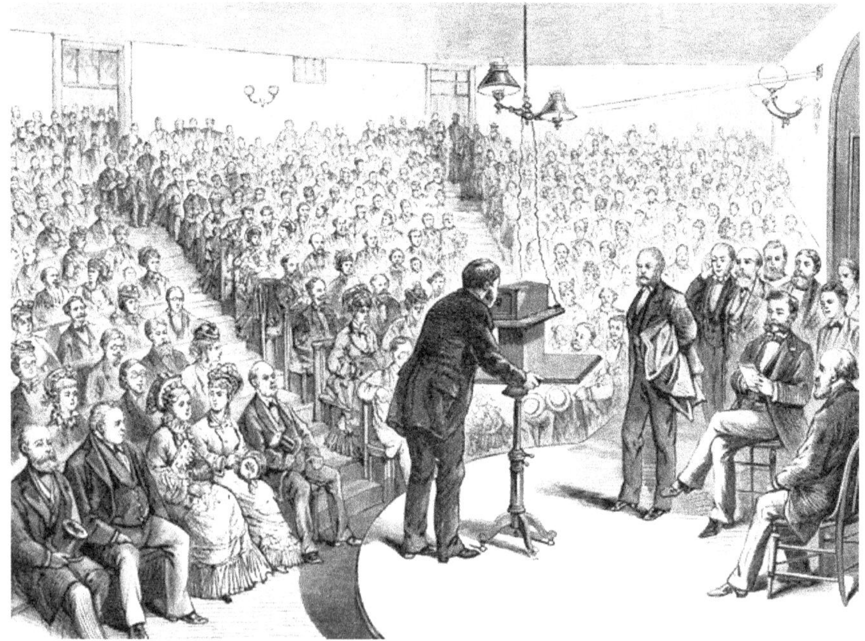

Alexander Graham Bell, who lived and worked in Salem during his early career, demonstrates the telephone at the Salem Lyceum. Some of his correspondence in the 1870s refers to Spiritualism.

where the Fox family lived. Everything was in flux and the potential for changing one's life seemed limitless.

Inventions such as the phonograph (1877), telephone (1876) and incandescent light bulb (1878) were of interest in Salem, with its long-established support of science and invention, and some were emblems of local pride. For example, Alexander Graham Bell conducted many of his early experiments while living in Salem and famously demonstrated the telephone at the Lyceum in February 1877. This was another area in which Salem could reassure itself of vitality and influence in national affairs.

In 1905, prolific author and native Salemite Mary Harrod Northend (1850–1926) published an article entitled "Salem of To-day":

> *The city of Salem.... is unique among the cities of America in that it has retained for so long its old, Colonial flavor, for it is only within the last thirty years that great changes have taken place in its "personnel"....*
>
> *Derby street, which was once the heart of the town in the halcyon days of the East India trade, is now peopled by the humble dwellers of the tenement house, while at the wharves, instead of ships full of costly treasures, now lie black coal barges, and schooners laden with lumber. At the east is the old training field (the Common) now called Washington Square, surrounded on all sides by graceful elms. Around this are built some of the finest residences of the city.*
>
> *Salem is now the centre of business for all the adjoining towns, being connected with them by railway and trolley lines. The busy throngs on the streets are a daily proof of this. Then, too, the town is constantly visited by the interested tourist, who is attracted here by the old houses, its witchcraft reputation, its museums, and most of all, because it was the birthplace of Nathaniel Hawthorne.*[22]

Salem, by the turn of the century, was a town still immersed in its past even as it tried to adjust to "great changes"...in its "personnel"—a change common in urban areas across America. A disastrous fire in 1914 challenged Salem to rise again, which it did, just as other cities, such as Boston and Chicago, did after their own great fires and San Francisco did after its earthquake.

Salem in the Gilded Age donned modern dress but clutched the comforting cloak of a mythologized glorious past firmly around its shoulders.

February 1892, Academy Hall

Let's return to that fire-lit room on the wintry night in 1892, as Mayor Rantoul takes the floor on the anniversary of the beginning of the witchcraft "delusion" in Academy Hall.

Rantoul began, "History imposes on us to-night a delicate and difficult task. We are here to commemorate something we would willingly forget. The witchcraft horror, the terrible frenzy which overtook our ancestors two centuries ago, is a chapter in our local annals which I for one would make haste to blot out forever if I had it in my power to do so."

After adding a few words of praise for those who had objected to the "frenzy," those who helped the accused to escape or those who had apologized and pointing out that "others elsewhere held the same beliefs" in witchcraft, he added that, nevertheless, "all this does not wipe out the appalling fact that right here in Salem at the hands of our own ancestors whom we honestly revere and hold up as better than their time in many ways, twenty innocent persons, mostly women, were by their own neighbors done to death."

> *I ask your attention, therefore, to what is about to be said…to record and hand down the actual fact and not expose our ancestors to the distorted misconceptions of writers who may not feel the solemn obligation resting upon us to see to it that the censure is apportioned to the fault. I shall rejoice if persons who have supposed us anxious to keep alive these memories for our own aggrandizement shall be persuaded by the solemnity of this occasion, that such is not the fact, and that while we cannot shape our history, we accept it in all seriousness as it is…the saddest of all episodes in the noble annals of a noble race.*[23]

Rantoul looked steadfastly out at his fellow Salemites and guests, then turned and introduced the next speaker, Barrett Wendell, professor of literature at Harvard College. What Wendell had to say was somewhat startling, and his conclusions would be argued about for years to come.

Chapter 2

Occult Incubators

No movement springs out like Athena from the head of Zeus, including Spiritualism. The 1848 communications with spirit worlds manifested by the Fox girls, from Hydesville, New York, most assuredly did not engender the "birth" of Spiritualism. To begin with, the region in which the Foxes lived was already called the "burned over district" due to its long history of extremist, evangelical or alternative religious enthusiasms.

In the same vein, the manifestations surrounding "bewitched" children in Salem in 1692, their behavior and the horrors that followed was not the "birth" of American participation or belief in witchcraft, the occult, or even severely dysfunctional neighborly relationships. These discrete events are perhaps more appropriately thought of as catalysts for wider dissemination and enlargement of older existing belief systems throughout the contemporary culture.

It is the intrinsic nature of human beings to construct narratives to make sense of the world and their place in it. The fear of the unknown is not easily overcome, and perhaps, it is more often than not only held at bay. The coping mechanisms human beings have devised to deal with the greatest unknowns—with death, with the unseen world beyond what the five senses reveal—have been particularly numerous and resourceful.

It's important to look beyond the proliferation of approaches we refer to as "occult" and treat each of them as historically rooted manifestations of the search for such fundamental first principles.

The aim of this chapter, then, is to help us construct a foundational understanding of key strands of the intricate web that contributed to the occult narratives operating regionally in nineteenth-century Salem and in the nation. We'll then have a better picture of the atmosphere that facilitated the adoption of Spiritualism and alternative practices falling outside established, mainstream American Judeo-Christian religion.

We'll be spending extended time on the influence of scientist and mystic Emanuel Swedenborg, since most of the other religious movements involved in the history of Spiritualism and the occult in Salem—indeed, throughout the world—are related to the theories he propounded.

Emanuel Swedenborg (1688–1772)

The opening paragraph on Pennsylvania's Swedenborg Foundation website teases us with: "What do William Blake, Ralph Waldo Emerson, Johnny 'Appleseed' Chapman, George Inness, Helen Keller, and D.T. Suzuki have in common? All were avid readers of the eighteenth-century Swedish scientist, nobleman, civil engineer, and religious visionary Emanuel Swedenborg. What attracted these prominent people, as well as numerous other poets, artists, writers, and people of faith to Swedenborg's spiritual writings?"

Swedenborg's own writings present a formidable challenge to answering that question. He was incredibly prolific; he wrote in Latin, and many of his works were not translated until late in the nineteenth century. The man himself seemed almost mythical, otherworldly, though he was very much a man of practical, concrete knowledge and scientific methodology.

"When it comes to Emanuel Swedenborg, it is hard to comprehend the sheer magnitude of his writings…His grasp was such that he anticipated many of the scientific breakthroughs of the nineteenth century in the fields of astronomy, metallurgy, magnetism, chemistry, atomic theory, and anatomy," John S. Haller wrote in the introduction to his excellent *Swedenborg, Mesmer, and the Mind/Body Connection: the Roots of Complementary Medicine.*[24]

Swedenborg's reputation for scientific accomplishment and methodology lent a certain authority to accounts of his clairvoyant, mystical and visionary experiences. His theological system was attractive to intellectuals, as well as to evangelically inclined religious reformists; this was an important aspect of the enduring influence he was to have.

Emanuel Swedenborg was born Emanuel Swedberg (or Svedberg) in Stockholm, Sweden, in 1688 (d. 1772, Julian calendar) to Jesper Swedberg

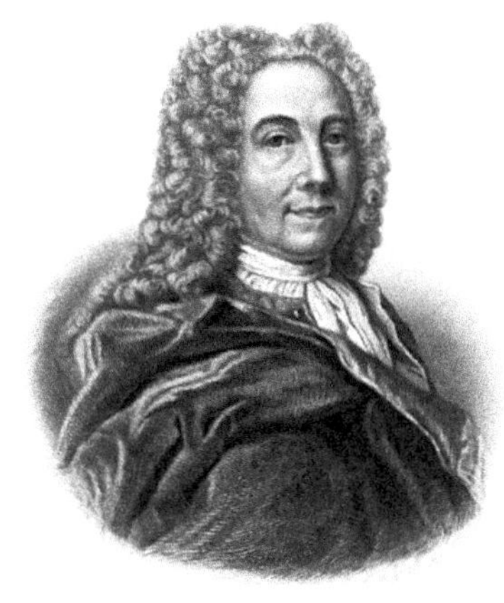
Emanuel Swedenborg.

(1653–1735) and Sara Behm (1666–1696). His clergyman father was also a professor of theology. A prodigy, he grew to young adulthood nurtured by an academically cultured and intellectually vibrant home atmosphere.

His early studies were theological, but by the time he had finished his studies at the University of Uppsala in 1709, he had moved on to a study of the physical sciences. At age twenty-two, Swedenborg traveled to London and Oxford, became involved in the scientific and religious debates of the day, attended the lectures of Sir Isaac Newton, wrote fables and designed a submarine, an air gun, a drawbridge, a flying machine and a musical instrument.

For most of his adult life, he held a seat in the Swedish House of Nobles, serving as the king's engineering advisor. A public service post supported him from 1724 to 1747. Throughout all this time, he became acquainted with most of the world's leading scholars.

In 1733, while Swedenborg was in Leipzig, he published a three-volume set of books, the first of which contained groundbreaking ideas. As John S. Haller describes it, "He postulated that the membranes and fluid constituting the human organism resonated with the auras in the universe...Energy was not something added to matter but was intrinsic in matter; energy actually was matter. With this concept, Swedenborg presaged the thinking on atomic particles and atomic energy by 200 years."

In the ensuing years, he began to grapple much more directly with questions about the natural world, attempting to find "physical traces of the soul." Over time, he became convinced that respiration was the central life-sustaining activity of the human body. He developed methods of concentration that relied on the "influx" of breath. Mystical sensibilities coupled with his scientist's mind led him into speculations about and studies of neurology and the brain, and some of his discoveries and theories were far ahead of his time.

Between 1743 and 1745, Swedenborg experienced a spiritual crisis, which led to visions and religious revelations. This profoundly changed the direction of his work. These mystical experiences served, for Swedenborg, to unify all the various strains of his intellectual and spiritual seeking. His metaphysical insights eventually formed the doctrinal basis of the New Jerusalem Church (or "New Church"). This New Church was seen as the culminating step to which Christianity must evolve.

Some recent scholarship on his life speculates that he may have, at some stages of his journey, been involved with Freemasonry and kabbalah. His language, however, throughout his writing remains firmly anchored and bound by Christianity. Rather too much so, thought Ralph Waldo Emerson (1803–1882), who complained in his own essay on Swedenborg, "The vice of Swedenborg's mind is its theological determination. Nothing with him has the liberality of universal wisdom, but we are always in a church." William James (1842–1910) had much the same reservation.

Following his revelatory experiences, Swedenborg entered into a kind of double existence. Though he went on with his business "in the world," privately he spent much of his time in "otherworldly" communication, "breathing inward to live" (i.e. using deep breathing to enter into a meditative state in a way that would seem familiar to modern yoga practitioners). In such a state, he could converse with angels, who apparently replicated human form. In this way, he obtained theological insights, which he poured into some forty works before his death in 1772.

Swedenborg wrote about "the nature of heaven and hell, regeneration, correspondences," and says Haller, "he likewise claimed to pass along messages from the dead received during visits to heaven…to have traveled beyond the solar system via the spiritual realms and conversed with the spirits residing on planets of distant suns."[25]

Swedenborgian concepts included the survival of a person's distinct, unique human personality after death; the veracity of earth-to-spirit communication; a hierarchal, intricately structured portrait of heaven and hell; and direct correspondence between the natural earthly world and the spiritual otherworld ("as above, so below").

In later years, he would travel with no attendant—his angel, he said, was always with him. On his land near Stockholm, he built a small house with a large garden featuring a wooden maze constructed for the enjoyment of visitors. One triangular building on this land contained three windows, and "when all of the doors were opened and mirrors placed in front of a fourth wall…three gardens were seen reflected…in the same order as in the original garden."[26] A nice bit of symbolism.

Swedenborg's explication of heavenly marriage, complete with sexual enjoyment, where truly loving couples would not only be reunited but would also enjoy full perfection of their ripened union ("Conjugal Love"), was the subject of some of his most intriguing (and controversial) writings. His ideas about the capacity for continued growth and progress of a soul before and after death to its most appropriate, most "comfortable" abode (be it heavenly or hellish) were directly influential on nineteenth-century Spiritualism.

Swedenborg's theories percolated through the world, undergoing the inevitable interpretive modifications and tropes. Swedenborgian theology came to America via converts and proselytizers, such as Scotsman James Glen (d. 1814), who brought New Church doctrines to Pennsylvania, Massachusetts, Virginia and Kentucky; publisher Francis Bailey (1744–1817), whose publications did much to foster interest in the church; booksellers who distributed New Church literature freely; and itinerant believers like John Chapman (1774–1845)—aka "Johnny Appleseed"—who spread Swedenborgian literature freely through the Midwest along with his apple seeds.

By the early 1800s, the first Swedenborgian church structure in the United States had been built, and a Swedenborgian, the Reverend John Hargrove (1750–1839), even preached in Washington, D.C., at the invitation of President Jefferson in 1802.[27]

Swedenborg in Salem

In the summer of 1794, William Hill, a boarder in Salem, made his "strong" beliefs in the "doctrines of Emanuel Swedenborg" known to all who would listen. Joseph Hiller, a silversmith who obtained the rank of major in the Revolutionary War and served as naval officer and collector of Salem[28] (appointed under Washington), became an early convert.

According to documents in the New Jerusalem Church Repository, for the years 1817 and 1818, "the number of readers increases in Salem…we have some powerful and excellent friends there."[29] The "New Church Society," aka the Church of the New Jerusalem or simply the Swedenborgian Church, sparked reading groups in private Salem homes by 1840; a small group of "but four persons" met at the home of a Mrs. Burleigh, on the corner of Washington and Lynde Streets.[30]

On July 24, 1844, however, when a grandson of Major Hiller, the Reverend O.P. Hiller, preached in Salem's Lyceum Hall, he was welcomed by an audience of "about four hundred people."[31] By 1861, meetings were

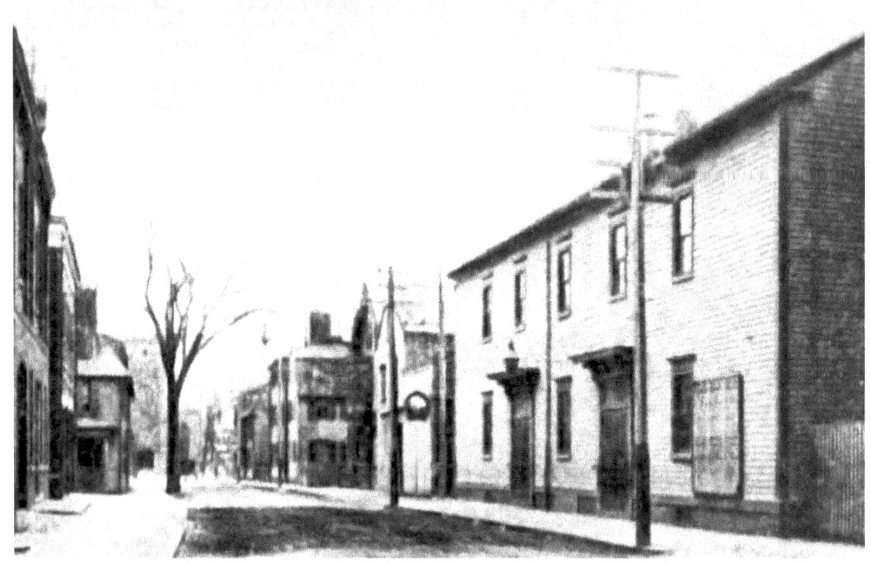

Lyceum Hall, circa 1892.

held in the former Henry Kemble Oliver schoolhouse on Federal Street. The groups moved around town for meetings, using Creamer Hall on Essex Street, Howard Street Church and Hamilton Hall.

According to Charles H. Webber and Winfield S. Nevins, writing in *Old Naumkeag: An Historical Sketch of the City of Salem, and the towns of Marblehead, Peabody, Beverly, Danvers, Wenham, Manchester, Topsfield, and Middleton* (1877):

> *In 1862, Rev. T.B. Hayward was invited to come to Salem, by the few people then interested in the "Heavenly Doctrines." As the result of his labors the "Salem Society of the New Jerusalem Church," consisting of thirteen members, was organized by him January 25, 1863. Mr. Hayward left the next year. Among his successors were the Rev. Abiel Silver, Rev. L. G. Jordan, and the present pastor, Rev. A. F. Frost.*[32]

Finally, in 1869, believers began to build a permanent structure for the Swedenborgian church. Dedicated in the spring of 1872, the church stood on Essex Street for some time but was "removed prior to 1906, when the Salem Athenaeum was built," according to authors Stephen J. Schier and Kenneth C. Turino, who published a photo of the church in their second volume of vintage Salem pictures. The church was modest, but the outside structure seems beautiful and dignified in photographs.

In 1877, according to Webber and Nevins, the church had thirty-four members and ran a "Sabbath School of forty children, the usual Sabbath congregation being about sixty." According to the *The History of Essex County* (1887):

> *April 1, 1884,…Rev. Duane V. Bowen was invited to become the minister of the society…Rev. Mr. Bowen was ordained in the Unitarian ministry in 1873, and had served parishes of that denomination before embracing the faith of the New Church and identifying himself with that body. In making the change he did not sever the bonds of friendship and sympathy by which he had been held in earlier fellowship…Of the fifty-nine original members of the New Church Society, twenty have removed from the city, and fourteen have been "removed to the spiritual world," the speech of this church not recognizing such translation as death.*[33]

Lectures on or congenial to New Church concepts were also given on the influential Salem Lyceum stage, indicating interest and curiosity in the general regional public beyond the dedication of devotees. For instance, during the eighteenth Lyceum course from 1846 to 1847, David H[atch] Barlow (1805–1864), a Unitarian minister and a friend of Emerson's, presented a talk entitled "Swedenborg."

Ralph Waldo Emerson's essay *Nature*, most often referred to as the defining document of the Transcendental movement, was strongly influenced by his readings of Swedenborg. As mentioned, Emerson also described the influential seer in the essay "Swedenborg; or, the Mystic" in his *Representative Men* (1850). Emerson was an exceedingly popular speaker on the Salem Lyceum platform, and although many found Transcendental ideas nearly incomprehensible or amusing, the perceptions of esoteric Transcendentalism must also be added to our picture of the "incubation period" for nineteenth-century Spiritualism in Salem.[34]

Folkloric Beliefs and Occult Knowledge

> *And now…I may be allowed the simple observation that superstition is a term broad and varied in its popular meaning and application…*

sometimes its operations have been misapprehended, and men have referred to its occurrences belonging rather to the departments of true science. Let us remember this; for there are mysteries in the loftiest regions of truth.[35]

We smile when we think of the witchcraft days in old Salem. The fact is, we are still living in those days. Not only do our country folk believe in signs and portents and omens, but trials for witchcraft are of not infrequent occurrence in this same State of Pennsylvania. And the people who place faith in these things supernatural are…sturdy farmers in a commonwealth that is reckoned as both prosperous and progressive…[36]

Throughout the centuries since 1692, Salem became synonymous with superstition, however prosaic the topic. The quote above, for example, linking Salem with witchcraft, signs and portents was taken from an article in a 1916 magazine that primarily discussed the need for modern scientific farming. The author believed farmers must bow to modern scientific truths, discarding folk practices such as planting in conjunction with the cycles of the moon. He was adamant: "We must get rid of the moon. It is one of the greatest obstacles in the way of agricultural efficiency."

Well. Getting rid of the moon is a tough proposition. Folk beliefs in occult, unseen external forces intervening in human life stubbornly persist because they satisfy some basic instinct, confirm concepts or simply because they satisfy tradition.

Certainly Essex County was typical in such beliefs, not just in the "old days," but also throughout the century we are examining. The earliest English settlers brought "white magic" and folk remedies with them; they saw no apparent contradiction with religion when they used a dowsing stick in search of water or employed herbs in curing rituals, for instance.

Since the area was primarily a maritime culture, seaborne superstitions abounded, and there was plenty of that flowing in with the tides. Yet Salem, despite its growth though the nineteenth century as a cosmopolitan area, also encompassed a bucolic, pastoral, gardening and farming region for a large stretch of its history. The rural folkloric concepts we examine here are as intrinsic to Salem as the sea lore of the North Shore.

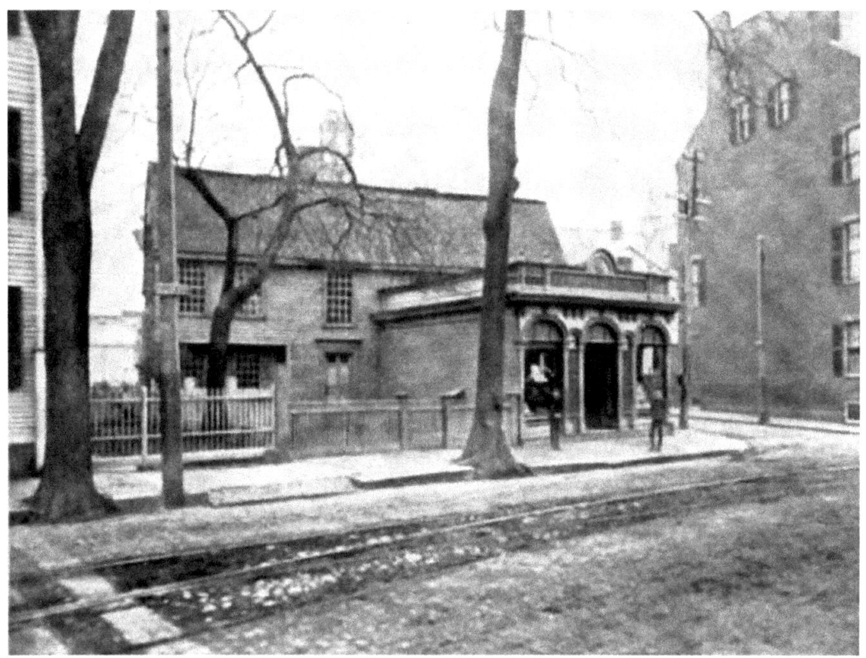

Corwin House, aka "Old Witch House," circa 1894.

Exotic Elements in Salem

In her memoir, Caroline Howard King underscores exoticism as a common element in the social fabric of Salem, a legacy of global shipping adventures, even outside museum walls. It was not unusual to see men dressed in Indian fabric walking downtown. Sandalwood scents emanated from warehouses and mixed with salt air. Foreign visitors inevitably brought with them alternative concepts of spirituality, provoking lively interest. A figure of Ganesha, the Indian lord of success and a symbol of Hinduism, watches over a doorway of the East India Marine Hall to this very day in modern Salem's majestic Peabody Essex Museum.

In a chapter entitled, "Ghost Stories of the North Shore,"[37] King outlines some of the regional beliefs in the supernatural:

> *When we first went to the Beverly Shore in 1840, the country people were of very primitive and unsophisticated race. No railroad had touched Beverly at that time, and the large freight of toll on the bridge kept them*

> *isolated from Salem, so that their intercourse with the outside world was limited to what grains of news they could glean from the driver of the stagecoach between Salem and Gloucester, which passed over their road twice a day.*
>
> *There were a few farmers on the shore...most of our neighbors were shoemakers and sailors, shoemaking in winter, and going to the Banks for fish in the summer. They were simple kindly friendly people—very superstitious, also, believing in all kinds of signs and omens...*
>
> *One morning while we were at the Farm I remember seeing an uncanny looking old black woman hobbling up the avenue, and when I asked the farmer's wife who she was, she said as naturally as if she had said—"she's a friend,"—"Oh she is a witch. She lives all alone by herself, and the neighbors say she has something called the Evil Eye and we are all afraid of her, although she never did us any harm, but I am always glad when she comes here to fill her basket with fresh eggs and other goods* [sic] *things just to get rid of her!"*
>
> *We found that these Beverly Shore people shared with their Marblehead neighbors their firm belief in the presence of spirits and supernatural appearances on their rocky shores...*
>
> *My Mother was born in Gloucester, and I wish I could remember all the quaint stories she used to tell us of the way her early life was guided by signs and omens...*[38]

King (who said witches were still spoken of with "bated breath" in Salem) described horseshoes hung over doors to repel evil and attract good luck and "large black bows on the beehives" to properly inform bees of a death in the family.

The Salem area harbored a strip of woods along the western border of town called "The Haunted Wood," and tales of local ghosts circulated during the antebellum years. One wonders about psychological connections to Salem's history of Quaker persecution, since early Quakers met in the woods on the western side of town.

We have already mentioned Joseph Story, associate justice of the U.S. Supreme Court, born September 18, 1779, in Marblehead (d. 1845). Story practiced law in Salem and became a prominent legal scholar. In 1851, his son, artist William Wetmore Story, fulfilled a filial duty by publishing books about his father's life and work. In the first volume, he described Marblehead's strange and wonderful atmosphere:

> *The main part of its population were sailors and fishermen, who, being drawn from all quarters of the globe, composed a strange heterogeneous society, having the customs, superstitions, and language of every country. Of all classes of persons sailors are the most credulous, and Marblehead was a sort of compendium of all varieties of legend. For instance, the belief in the Pixies of Devonshire, the Bogles of Scotland, and the Northern Jack o'Lanthorn was prevalent there;—and my father has told me, that he was often cautioned by the fishermen, just at twilight, to run home, or the Bogles would be sure to seize him. Mystery was in the air; signs and tokens were drawn from the most trivial occurrences...*

His father's own autobiographical notes confirm these anecdotes and describe other strange occult local characters.

> *Among the inhabitants of the town were many peculiar characters...Among them was an eccentric and perverse man of secluded habits, of considerable study, and of great natural sagacity, whom the townsfolk nicknamed, Uncle Dimond. Scarcely any of the humbler people in Marblehead had a doubt that he was "in league with the devil," as they expressed it...numberless are the stories which I have heard told to prove his supernatural powers.*[39]

This famous "uncle" had an even more famous offspring: a Lynn seeress named Mary "Moll" Pitcher. In an account of Moll's prophecies, published in 1895, we find more descriptions of Dimond:

> *Her grandfather, old Captain Dimond, was called the "Wizzard of Marblehead," and it was said: "Used to pace the cemetry* [sic] *at night conversing with ghosts and witches and his voice could be heard miles out at sea directing the course of vessels."*
>
> *Those were superstitious times, not far removed from the hypnotic influence of Parris over the fair maids of Salem, whose disordered vision made them see the flying witches on broom sticks, instead of bicycles.*
>
> *Captain Dimond claimed to have descended from a race of famous astrologers. He boasted his grandparent could cast as good a horoscope as any Arabian, Greek or Egyptian of the 13th century.*
>
> *So, if he chanced to be out conversing with his starry friends, his earthly ones said it was with "Ghosts and Witches." And if presaging a storm, should turn out and use his stentorian voice in sailor fashion, to prevent ships entering the Cove from being dashed upon the innumerable rocks there.*[40]

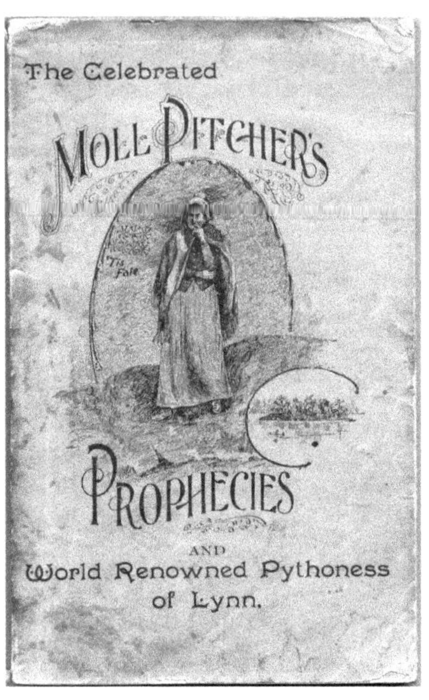

The famous "Moll" and her prophecies.

Dimond's own descendant, Mary "Moll" Pitcher (circa 1738–1813), is quite possibly the most famous seer in the years leading up to the nineteenth century on the North Shore, perhaps in all of regional history. The memory of her proclaimed psychic abilities potently supported belief in human capability to connect and channel unseen forces. In her cottage on High Rock, Lynn, she was consulted by people of all stations and walks in life hoping to benefit from her extraordinary visionary skills. She often presented her prophecies in rhymes, similar to oracles of previous centuries.

As to her accuracy, James Robinson Newhall (1809–1893), a justice in the police court of Lynn, but better known as a historian of his town, remarks, "It cannot be denied that her predictions were verified oftentimes with almost startling exactness, and acute reasoners have been most painfully exercised in attempting to account for her extraordinary success on any known principles."

Newhall speaks of her with respect in his "Lecture on the Occult Sciences," published in 1845: "That she was an extraordinary woman, cannot be doubted…Few could read the human heart with such precision; and few could with such unerring certainty discover a true index to the affections, the hopes, the fears, of others, in a trembling word, a transient glance. Her influence was felt throughout the civilized world; and fortunes and honors were secured or lost through her predictions.[41]

One of Moll's neighbors, a Dr. Burchstead, had made an arched gate of bones from a beached whale over the posts leading to his house; it is said that neighbors shy of being known as seekers of occult knowledge used a desire to see the whale bones as a convenient excuse for seeking her cottage "on the road to Salem."[42]

A July 15, 1879 *New York Times* article, reprinted from the *Boston Traveller*, gives evidence of Moll's long-lasting fame and cultural influence. The article accurately described her as a young and beautiful woman who dressed well and was intelligent, quick and who "ambled like a frisky colt" up to the age of seventy.

Unfortunately, the article, while paying tribute to Moll's astute reading of human character and success as a fortuneteller, also claimed she was a thief who supplied the two large pockets of her dress liberally from the local store. Moll, according to this article, used her young daughter to imitate the noise of the "chained devil" ostensibly kept upstairs in the house to frighten and intimidate seekers who were slow to pay for their tea readings. Sometimes the fortune read for the sitter reflected Moll's annoyance over a perceived slight. This 1879 account differed from earlier accounts of her character, which had never previously been so assailed.

> *Aye, thrilling are the legend tales connected with this mound,*
> *And superstitious multitudes still think it hallowed ground,*
> *Old matrons to their children in raptures now will talk*
> *How Molly told their fortunes once at "Old High Rock."*[43]

The table at which Moll had, according to legend, told fortunes was even displayed in the museum rooms of the august Essex Institute, according to a late nineteenth-century Salem visitor's guide. Stories of Moll in her prognosticating perch above the sea permeated regional historical memory and attracted seekers to the site of such strong spiritual "energy." Her old abode, High Rock in Lynn, was to become even more famous as a site of spiritualist power, especially due to its use by members of the Hutchinson Family Singers.

The Hutchinsons were the most popular American singing ensemble of the antebellum and Civil War eras. Zealous social reform advocates, they were active from the 1840s to the 1880s. Jesse Hutchinson Jr. (1813–1853), who wrote much of the group's material and managed its affairs, built a house on the property, following clairvoyant advice. Subsequently, he erected a tower as well. The site became a retreat for traveling Spiritualists of all kinds.

After his death in 1853, Jesse was reported in publications such as the *Spiritual Telegraph* to have returned in séances, not only leading Hutchinson family songs for those assembled but also apparently composing new tunes from beyond the veil and sending them through mediumistic channels.

Abby Hutchinson Patton (1829–1892), who largely confined her activities to performing while the troupe was active, later became particularly known for arrangements of African American spirituals, her hymn "Kind Words

Can Never Die" (1855) and "Ring Out, Wild Bells" (1891), a setting of Tennyson's Christmas poem. Abby reportedly also made her postmortem appearances at séances, even giving love advice to those present.

Famed seer Andrew Jackson Davis (1826–1910) attended what he termed a "Spiritual Congress" from High Rock tower. In his vision, he received visits from representatives of two dozen nations of the world (in spirit form)—a sort of United Nations Assembly of the air.[44]

In 1853, Universalist minister, abolitionist, activist and Spiritualist John Murray Spear (1804–1887), after receiving his own visionary messages on High Rock, worked with permission on the Hutchinsons' grounds to build his electrical "God Machine" (aka "New Motive Power") with the assistance of his spirit guides, among them a "Band of Electricizers," led by Benjamin Franklin. This rather bizarre construction was intended to bring a New Messiah into the world as "Heaven's last, best gift to man."

Mesmerism/Animal Magnetism: Franz Anton Mesmer (1734–1815)

Science and religion in the nineteenth century were not the strange bedfellows we tend to think of them as today in our post–"monkey trial" era. Spiritualism, most particularly, was touted as a religion rooted in progress and science.

The second major influence on the development of Spiritualism was animal magnetism or mesmerism. The theories and practices of animal

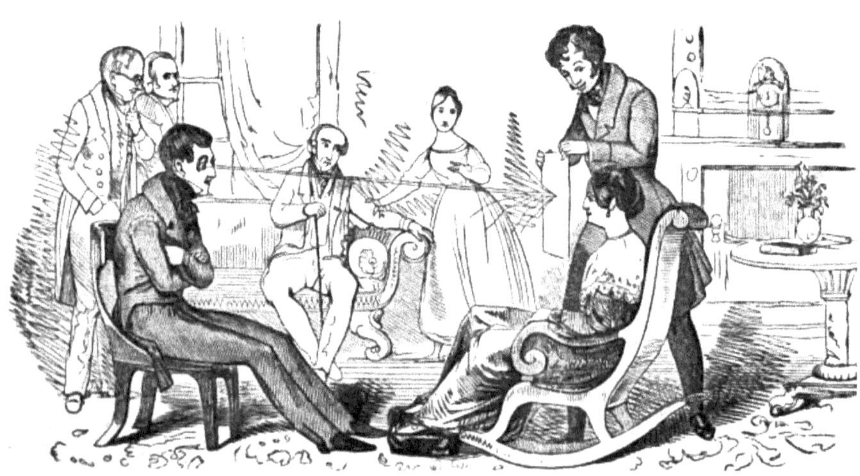

magnetism or mesmerism, though controversial in their time, can be understood as rooted in medical science, precursors to the development of therapeutic hypnotism. Of course, the same practices also supplied hypnotic hijinks in entertaining or dramatic stage demonstrations.

Both the serious scientific intent and the dramatic public flourish were present in the character and work of Franz Anton Mesmer.

Magnetic Medicine

In experimenting with methods to treat his patients, Mesmer eventually came to describe animal magnetism as a kind of vital fluid, an energy, which, though invisible, was present in all creation; this vital fluid, he theorized, could pass between patient and doctor during treatments to affect cures. The effect on the human body was "analogous to the magnet."

Illness resulted from a deficiency or imbalance in animal magnetism, and the doctor's ability to restore the free flow of such vitality personally and directly to the patient was a key component of the treatment. One fundamental cause of illness dictated one fundamental restorative.

Although the practice developed some bizarre elements as time went on, Mesmer trained as a serious physician (albeit of immense ego and a flair for the dramatic). He earned a doctorate of medicine in 1766 from the University of Vienna. Mesmerism was a secular method rather than religious and touted a scientific theoretical basis initially inspired by Mesmer's interest in the work of Isaac Newton (1642–1727) and Johannes Kepler (1571–1630).

Born in Iznang, a village in Baden-Württemberg, Germany, Mesmer studied theology and law in his youth and earned a doctorate in philosophy as well as the degree in medicine already mentioned. His practice took him to Vienna, France and Switzerland, although he spent the last years of his life back on the shores of Lake Constance.

After marriage to a wealthy widow shortly after receiving his medical degree, Mesmer lived a cultured life in Vienna, practicing medicine. He was a noted patron of the arts in whose private theater Wolfgang Amadeus Mozart's earliest opera was performed and to which other famous musicians flocked. Mesmer himself played the glass harmonica.[45] Music, importantly, was usually a component of the treatment atmosphere for his healing sessions.

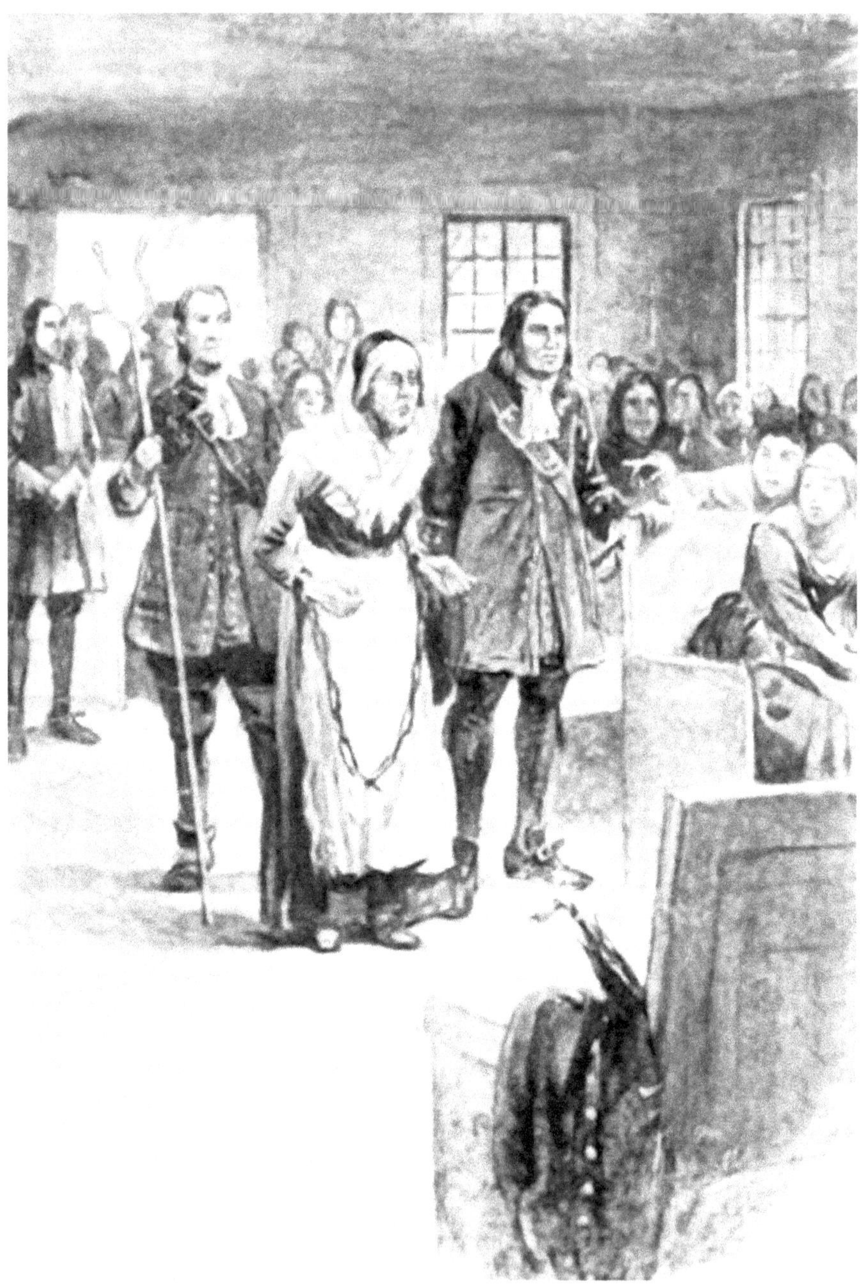

Illustration from *The Witch of Salem; or, Credulity Run Mad*, by John R. Musick.

Mesmer took on patients who were "difficult": they had exhausted or could not be helped by conventional medical treatments. Most were suffering from what was discernibly an emotional or psychological illness. Mesmer could point to cures through his methods.

Unfortunately, his reputation unraveled when he could not convince the European medical establishment those methods were, indeed, sound, and he fled at least one city under mysterious circumstances—possibly because a "cure" had reversed itself. Afterward, Mesmer founded a society to continue work in the field of animal magnetism. However, his unfortunate proclivity to mold this society into a personal cult, with all monies accruing to him, further discredited him.

Among society members was one of Salem's most famous visitors: the Marquis de La Fayette, who attempted to introduce mesmerism to America via recommendations to George Washington (much to the disgust of Thomas Jefferson, who was happy when the "maniac Mesmer" fell from grace).

Yet he had converts and followers. Significantly, some disciples found that, when they magnetized patients, those patients fell into an altered state of consciousness resembling sleep (they were "mesmerized"). In this condition, they displayed "extraordinary lucidity," clairvoyance, precognition and other unusual abilities while concurrently displaying a kind of apathy and seeming inability to experience pain. The anesthetic aspect of mesmeric trance was put to use in operations such as tooth extractions.

In Europe, the use and discussion of mesmerism was mostly confined to elite circles and within well-defined institutional boundaries. In the United States, animal magnetism was introduced to the populace as a whole, with the large middle class its primary audience, and demonstrations took place on stages and other public forums rather than in private institutions.

A Frenchman, Charles Poyen St. Sauveur (d. 1844), former abolitionist, evangelical Christian and later self-proclaimed professor of animal magnetism, toured New England in 1836. He introduced Americans to the new science from the lecture hall and other public stages. He would often call for volunteers from the audience, ensuring an element of entertainment for the curious, but his intent was serious. He believed that mesmerism or animal magnetism was a natural force, not a supernatural one. Poyen was fond of making a martyr's lament when he encountered opposition—which, of course, he did.

Spotlight: Andrew Jackson Davis (1826–1910)

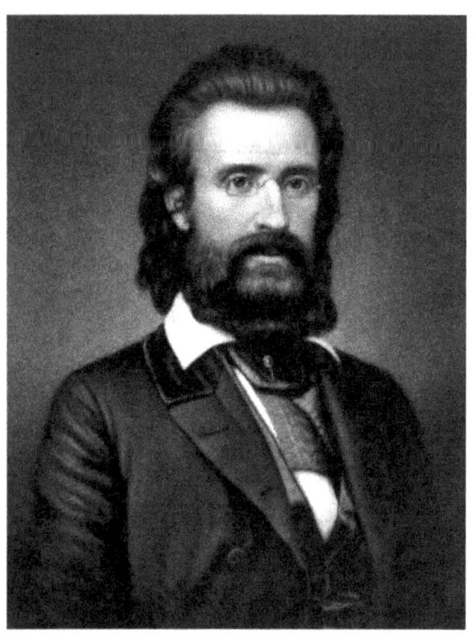

The phenomenally prolific Andrew Jackson Davis.

Through the public demonstrations of mesmerism, many were introduced to the "realities" of spirit communication and clairvoyance, which was, as noted, a talent frequently displayed by those in a "mesmeric trance."

Just such a subject was Andrew Jackson Davis. Young Davis traveled around, giving demonstrations with his magnetizer, a musician from Bridgeport named Dr. Lyon, and the Reverend William Fishbough, who operated as transcriptionist of Davis's early trance revelations.

When he found he could mesmerize himself, without his "handlers," his career truly began. He developed visions in which, he claimed, he had become a personal "initiate" of Emanuel Swedenborg (postmortem). Though Davis claimed to be untutored, he published scores of influential, complicated books about the spirit world, descriptions of other worlds he visited throughout the universe, prophecies and revelations.

Davis wrote over thirty books; his *Great Harmonia*, published in five volumes, established an enduring blueprint of Spiritualist cosmology. Significantly, he had little use for organized, sectarian religion. Davis metamorphosed into perhaps the most important of many proselytizers and practitioners of Spiritualism in America.

After Dr. George Bush, professor of Hebrew at the University of New York observed Davis and witnessed him, in trance states, using Hebrew (which Davis ordinarily did not know), he became an enthusiastic supporter of the seer, publishing his praise. Although Bush later tempered his opinions, the support of such prominent, educated men did much to bolster the spread and acceptance of Spiritualism.

Poyen and Mesmerism in Salem

During his tour of New England, Poyen resided in various cities for short durations, including Salem, and he was careful to collect and publish supportive letters and articles from newspapers to bolster the acceptance of his cause. In his book *Progress of Animal Magnetism in New England*, he quoted a testimonial from the *Salem Gazette* of August 11, 1837:

> *I allude to the experiments performed at Danvers, on Saturday evening last, by our well-known, sincere, and intellectual townsman, Mr. J. Dixon.*
>
> *"Mr. D. first tried his art upon a girl about eight years of age, resident in Salem. She was placed in a chair, opposite, and within a few feet of Mr. D., who calmly folded his arms, and with his eyes fixed intently upon her, sat perfectly still. He requested that silence might be preserved among the audience—not that it would affect her, but would distract his own attention…*
>
> *After a sitting of ten minutes, the girl was apparently asleep. The first object was to satisfy the audience that the sleep was supernatural. Accordingly, she was placed so that all could see and handle, and be convinced. To this end, noises were made equivalent to the discharge of a fowling-piece close by her, but not a muscle moved. Her hands were deadly cold. They might be pinched to discoloration, but no movement indicated the least sensation. Mr. D. then willed her, (without speaking,) to raise her hand. Instantly, it was convulsed and slowly raised. He then, placing in her hand a closed penknife, at the same time conveying the idea to her that it was an apple, bade her eat it. Again were the convulsive motions visible, she raised her hand until it came in contact with her mouth.*
>
> *…After repeating similar experiments, he willed her to awake. Convulsed in every limb, she slowly, slowly awoke…Several minutes elapsed before she was able to walk; her first convulsive attempt at which, conveyed forcibly the idea of a departed spirit returning to reanimate a corpse already stiffened in death.*
>
> *…I subsequently asked her how she felt. She replied that she "liked it,"—but when it was coming on, she felt as if spiders were creeping all over her, and sometimes rather cold;—she could remember nothing that transpired during the slumber, and on awaking was bright and well as ever…"*[46]

Joseph Dixon (1799–1869) was an inventor, chemist, printer and optician who ran a Salem business from 1827 to 1847. Dixon's company later pioneered the industrial use of graphite and was famous for grinding lenses, among other scientific and photographic accomplishments. Henry David Thoreau's father learned to make pencils in Dixon's shop. The company, now called the Dixon Ticonderoga Company, still makes its famous pencils.

More testimonials specifically from Salem, from individuals important to the town's later history, were included in Poyen's book:

> *The Letter which we are going to place before the eyes of the reader, is from Dr. Jos. E. Fisk, of Salem, one of those men, whose countenance, language, and manners, express so great simplicity of heart, benevolence and honesty, that I should consider it almost a crime to charge him with concerting a plan with any person to deceive his fellow-creatures. Dr. Fisk has made, with the greatest success, several series of experiments, which has been the means of convincing a great number of the most respectable citizens of Salem, of the reality of Animal Magnetism.*
>
> *Salem, Oct. 22d, 1837*
> *"Dr. Ch. Poyen—"My Dear Sir,—You wish me to state in a few lines, the result of my experiments in Animal Magnetism….*
>
> *I began to occupy myself with it, only since you have come among us, and my professional occupations taking most of my time, I have experimented upon but few individuals. I have, however, obtained some results which have confirmed me in the opinion that the subject is not all a delusion, as a great many pretend it to be, but is one which is well worthy of a thorough investigation by scientific men. I have succeeded in producing well-marked effects on three persons…*
> *…At your request, I will certify that I have not yet seen any ill effects, either moral or physical, follow any of my experiments. I am very truly yours, Jos. E. Fisk."*[47]

We will meet Dr. Fisk [*sic*] again. Poyen claimed for the "mission" of mesmerism other prominent citizens of Salem (including a lawyer), some of whom declined to be named in print but who were "well known" to be practitioners.

After Poyen returned to France in 1839, Englishman Robert Hanham Collyer (1814–c.1891) began his own American lecture tour, originally hoping to promote phrenology. Bradley University professor of religious studies Robert C. Fuller tells us, "The diary he kept and later published

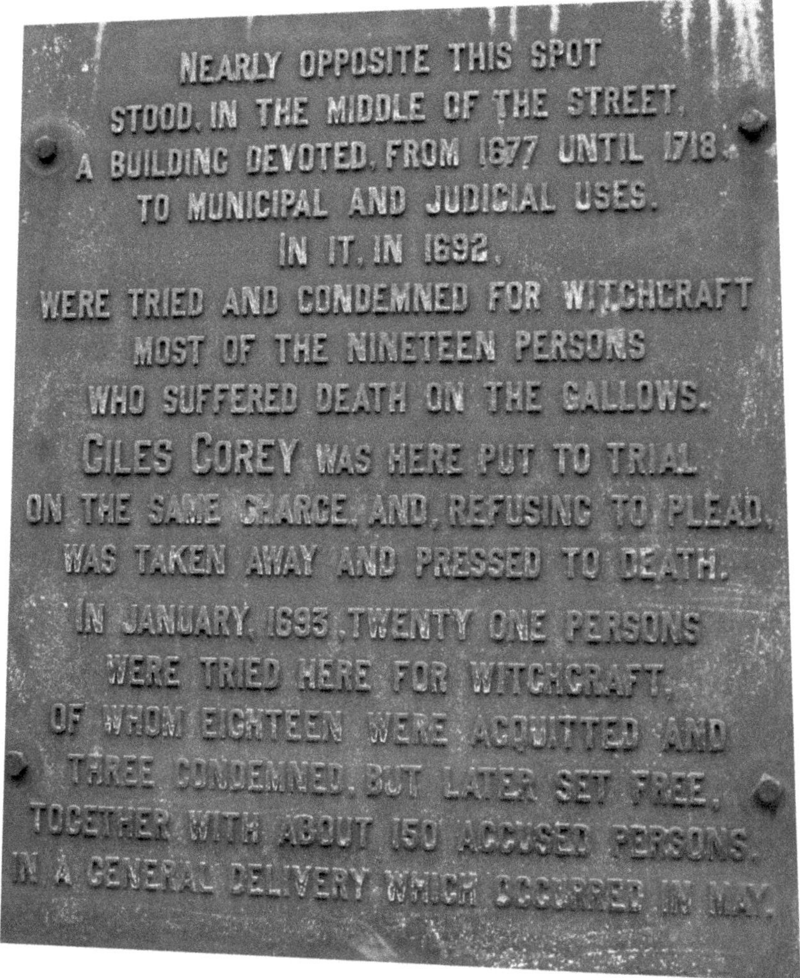

Silent witnesses to the past are everywhere in Salem.

under the title *Lights and Shadows of American Life* does for early American psychology what de Tocqueville did for American democracy. From the perspective of an outsider, he offers succinct observations of the period's cultural landscape to help explain why particular conceptions of human nature were able to gain such a strong foothold."[48]

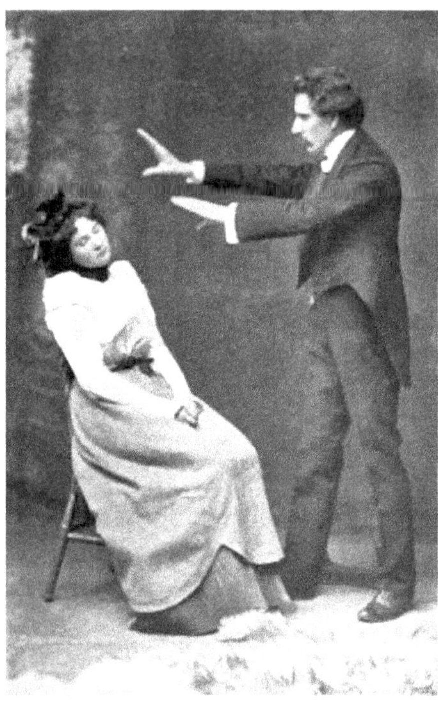

Woman as sleeping subject and man as mesmerist was a configuration and an image that troubled some.

The early reaction in Salem, where a sophisticated scientific attitude was a point of pride, was often skeptical. Although Salem, and the rest of the world, understood there were indeed real, if invisible forces, in the natural world such as electricity and gravity and that new discoveries continued, many scoffed publicly at the claims made for mesmerism's healing power.

Derisive letters and commentary were sent to the Salem press or reprinted from other newspapers. The man, quoted above, who signed himself "F" and described Dixon's experiments, found himself defending his observations to mocking correspondents. One lengthy reaction began, "What are we coming to?" and claimed, tongue-in-cheek, that a dream placed them in Salem of 2837, where they read in the *Salem Gazette* of commonplace events such as a person "thrown into a ten hour magnetic sleep and whisked away to Mars" and other such fantasies. The letter ended sardonically with another imagined news item from this futuristic scene—that a thief had entered a bank, placed the teller into magnetic sleep and "made off with 20,000 dollars."

Another wag in the August 15, 1837 *Salem Gazette* signed their satiric sendup of mesmerism "A Wolf In Sheep's Clothing." "F's" reply to this critic, printed on the twenty-second of that month, was detailed and elaborate and underlined the factual, not metaphysical, nature of mesmerism and "magnetic sleep."

Yet the metaphysical would inevitably enter; as the science of animal magnetism developed in America, it meshed with and interacted with the growing religious and reformist restlessness of the antebellum years and seemed to promise those who hungered for the religious ecstasies of the

Second Great Awakening a way to relive those experiences. Mesmerism became a tool for "healing the soul" by harmonizing the body.

Since medical diagnosis and treatment was, to put it kindly, somewhat haphazard, using mesmerism or animal magnetism as a form of medical practice did seem worth exploring to some in mid-century America, and certainly, in Salem.

Masons, Oddfellows and Fraternities

Mention should also be made of the long-standing secret societies that existed in Salem by the nineteenth century. Of the various and numerous fraternal organizations that populated Old Naumkeag, the Masons, in particular, had deep roots. The Essex Lodge, F.A.M., dated from March 9, 1779, under authority for the Massachusetts Grand Lodge "descending from the Grand Master of Scotland." With some interruptions, more lodges appeared throughout the years, and by 1879, there were six "branches of the Masonic fraternity."[49]

This is significant to our story because, according to historian Mark C. Carnes's study of ritual in American Victorian fraternal organizations, an important change occurred in the character of groups such as the Masons, Odd Fellows and Red Men during the antebellum years.

Formerly a social club for "merry" fellowship in the eighteenth century, the societies subsequently developed highly ritualized ceremonies, as well as esoteric and religious didacticism. Members were bound to secrecy and made "attempts to recreate the primitive 'Masonry' of the ancient Egyptians, Druids, Persians, Eleusinians, or Kabbalists."[50] These esoteric rituals were conducted, largely, by men operating, in ordinary life, in positions of trust and community influence. The secret societies also fostered anti-mainstream religious impulses:

> *By mid-century the rituals of American Freemasonry and Odd Fellowship had been completely transformed: references to man's goodness had been replaced with an assumption of his innate sinfulness; approval of his innocent enjoyment of life's pleasures with a "dreadful track" of trials and tortures; a solicitous God with an "awful being"…*
>
> *The ritualists of the 1840s and 1850s established the theological foundation for the rituals that proliferated during the last third of the 19th*

century...the rituals of all major and most minor orders offered a form of religious expression far removed from the liberal beliefs which had come to prevail in the churches of the middle classes.[51]

Visionary Religions

Two religious sects that honor "visionary revelation" as key to their theological structures were influential on the overall culture that produced Spiritualism: the United Society of Believers in Christ's Second Appearing (the Shakers) and Mormons.

Shaker elders specifically named Swedenborg as their "John the Baptist." The religious beliefs and practices of the Shakers, like Swedenborg's, can be seen as antecedents to Spiritualism. Salem visitors to Shaker villages included Reverend William Bentley, who detailed his visits with his usual eye for detail and care for personal attributes, and Nathaniel Hawthorne.

Hawthorne's reactions evolved each time he visited, and his feelings about the sect were complex. Nevertheless, he wrote several stories as a result of his explorations.

Salem's experience with Mormonism also forms an intriguing chapter in the religious life of Old Naumkeag.

The United Society of Believers in Christ's Second Appearing (The Shakers)

Four dead babies.

Such sorrowful seeds to bloom into song, dance and a religious movement that, at high tide, embraced thousands of people.

The Shaker story is replete with riddle and paradox, contrast and conundrum. There's Ann Lee Standerin (1736–1784) herself, central to the American Shaker foundational story: a blacksmith's daughter, her budding youth imprisoned in the industrialized workplaces of grimy Manchester, England.

A woman who labeled the marriage bed a "bed of embers." A bereft mother, who had, early Shaker histories claimed, buried four tiny babies (although modern scholarship can find documentation of only one). In *Shakers. Compendium of the origin, history, principles, rules and regulations, government, and doctrines of the United Society of Believers in Christ's Second Appearing. With biographies of Ann Lee, William Lee, Jas. Whittaker, J. Hocknell, J. Meacham, and Lucy Wright (1859)*, Shaker elder Frederick William Evans (1808–1893) sketched a portrait of "Mother" Ann Lee:

> *Many called her beautiful…She possessed a sound, strong, and healthy physical constitution, and remarkable powers and faculties of mind. At times, when under the operation of the Holy Spirit, her form and actions appeared to be divinely beautiful and angelic. The power and influence of her spirit was then beyond description, and she spoke as "one having authority."*[52]

Clay for Christ in female form? Many disciples believed so.

Illiterate Ann Lee could sign her marriage certificate with only her mark—yet generations of disciples named her "Ann the Word of God Made Manifest in the World" or, more simply, "Ann the Word."

Celibate Ann Lee: "Mother" to thousands.

In the post–English Civil War era, options for religious answers and new spiritual paths abounded. The Manchester area during Ann's day, according to University of California Comparative Religions and Research professor Catherine L. Albanese, harbored Swedenborgians as well as ecstatic sects known as the "French Prophets" or Camisards.[53]

Ann Lee's religious search rested with "the Shaking Quakers," or "Shakers." The Shaking Quakers were a plain, simple people, yet they experienced "Vapours in Ekstatick Fits" and disturbed neighbors during worship services by screeching "in the most dreadful manner." They sang and danced as the spirit moved them, to the point of exhaustion.

Ann Lee soon established herself as a dedicated and devout member of the sect. Into the emptiness of heart engendered by grief, she poured the fervor of delighting in God.

Surmising that sexual use of the body had led her astray, among her religious convictions was the necessity of celibacy. Such behavior, if rigorously maintained, was the straight and narrow way to God, she proclaimed.

She and her fellow Shakers endured the traditional wages of pious radicalism: prosecutions and persecutions, imprisonments and indignities. Their missionary work in England reached a saturation point; new fields for proselytization were desired. Ann Lee and her followers looked west.

In early August 1774, a mustard seed–sized group of English transplants disembarked from a harrowing trip across the sea in a dilapidated ship. Their first settlement was called by its Indian name, *Nisqueunia* (or *Niskeyuna*). Leaders Ann Lee, William Lee and James Whittaker guided the nascent United Society of Believers in Christ's Second Appearing through its incubation period. Curious about these "strange people" in the isolated village, others came, watched and listened. Some converted. Leaders dispersed to carry the message to other locales.

Few contemporaries could come away from observing them without strong opinion; few could remain complacent in contemplation of the Shakers self-described apostolic mission. All preconceptions were challenged, not the least startling of which was belief in Ann Lee as the female manifestation of Christ. The Shakers sent a familiar message in one respect, however. Much as other sectarian religions did and still do, they purported to return their followers to the pure forms of early and original Christianity.

Worship rituals privileged the oral over the written. They rejected established ecclesiastical structure and resisted formal theological formulae. They set an example by constant living devotion: labor was worship, worship was labor. Life was perfected by this symbiosis. Shakers communicated with the spirit world through visions and dreams, and spirits guided them in devising new rituals for worship and communication on the earthly plane.

The Shakers danced and laughed, groaned and turned, whirled and hopped. Songs were woven into every aspect of the everyday tasks of life. That dancing, singing, movement and work were all seamless components of worship was, to them, no innovation. In the Shaker view, it was a return to deep understanding, to primal sources.

Their songs were received, they felt, in a straight-sluice conduit from God. The Shakers called them "gifts." The key here, as it would be for other sects, was love. Shakers early on, through ecstatic visions, music and "gifts," were in touch with the spirit world, always understood as love.

In 1837, these spirit communications took such a fervent turn that, Albanese tells us, "members of the United Society of Believers...called this the Era of Manifestations..."

> *The inaugural series of ecstatic visitations echoed in a different key the possession stories of the mostly teenage girls who in 1692 began the notorious Salem witchcraft episode. Now at Watervliet, New York, three girls aged between 10 and 14 fell under a power that Shakers linked to the work of the Holy Spirit and, alternately, to Mother Ann...* [One girl] *had traveled, she reported, with a spirit sister into the City of Paradise, with its four hundred buildings set in four rows. She...had also seen Jesus and Mother Ann.*

> *Before a month had passed, the spirit visitations were multiplying… "In these wonderful days," wrote a member of the New Lebanon ministry, the dead "generally and frequently return in spirit, and minister comfort and consolation to their surviving friends"…*
>
> *So it was that mediums—or, as the Shakers called them, "instruments"—who felt themselves to be in communication with spirits, became important ritual leaders in Shaker communities, where worship already involved forms of sacred dance and ecstatic behavior.*[54]

Shaker elders specifically linked the revelations and spiritual work done during the years in America with the later manifestations at the Fox home in Hydesville, New York.

American Shaker theology became more intricate during the era of "Mother Ann's Work," as it was also called, but two aspects of their practice should remain with us as we approach the birth of "modern" Spiritualism: the importance and the leadership of women, especially as clairvoyant "instruments," and the belief that communication with those in the spirit world (i.e. the dead) was not only possible, but also part of the natural fabric of life.

Salem's Connections with the Shakers

In his journal for the summer of 1795,[55] William Bentley wrote:

> *On Saturday I rode from Harvard five miles to Shirley to see the settlements of a sect called Shakers. They are more easily described by their modes of life, than by any doctrines they retain…I saw it in its infancy, & attended the lectures of one of its elders…His address was ready, & his manner not unlike the common rant of our New Lights.*[56] *He had no distortions, but his hearers being about 16 men & 25 women, were greatly agitated, particularly in the confused singing, or noise called labouring…*

Bentley related that they were "kindly received," by all and visited the meetinghouse, though due to the absence of the community's spiritual elder, he could ask few questions about doctrine. The meetinghouse was notable not only for its neatness, but also for the main room, where the "moveable benches" enabled them to set it up "clear like a Dancing Room."

Bentley's group was also received kindly in Harvard. The minister noted that the celibate Shakers left the future of their religion to God, trusting to "proselytism."[57]

In Salem newspapers, advertisements for Shaker goods, such as brooms and herbal remedies, were frequent by mid-century; so wholesome Shaker work was certainly appreciated in town. Yet Shaker ways of being did not find universal approbation.

In 1841, for instance, an article was republished in the *Salem Gazette* from the *Worcester Aegis* entitled "Interesting Case." The story involved one Nancy Brown, who appeared in the Court of Common Pleas as "a bright-eyed and intelligent girl of fifteen, in the prim garb and exceeding purity of the Shaker costume."

Nancy had been "placed" with the Shakers by her former master, Nathaniel Chandler, Esq., for "some reasons of private convenience" before her term of servitude with him expired. She acclimated to the Shakers' supportive community and was treated as family. When Nancy's reprobate parents visited her, she told them they were strangers (as surely they must have seemed to her).

Brown wanted to remain with the Shakers, whose feelings were mutual, the relationships affectionate; nevertheless, legal proceedings were instituted to remove her from the influence of the "sterile creed." During arguments, onus was laid against her master, Chandler, for placing the child in an "isolated community, holding strange and unnatural opinions"—a danger to the child since "if she could be secluded that way with the Shakers, she might also be shut up in a convent, or placed in charge of the Mormons." The result was that it was "deemed inexpedient" to return her to the Shakers. As she was a minor, she was sent to another home in town to await final decisions in her care.

Thus, it can be seen, parallels with the Shaker way of life were drawn to two other "suspect" religions: Roman Catholicism and Mormonism.

Mormons in Salem

Of all the odd episodes in Salem's long history, perhaps one of the oddest is the town's early connection to the Mormon church.

Ancestors of Joseph Smith Jr. (1805–1844), founder of the sect, settled in Topsfield in 1638, and the first Samuel Smith, son of Robert, the original emigrant from England, "was among the accusers of a witch at the famous trials" in Salem.[58]

The nineteenth-century Joseph Smith was another product of the "burned-over district" in New York state. Again it should be remembered that that area of the country at the time of the founding of Smith's visionary religion was part of frontier America, a region by definition in the throes of evolving identity. Joseph's family had moved from tenant farm to tenant farm throughout his childhood in Vermont, New Hampshire and, finally, Manchester, New York; this unsettled childhood must be considered in any retelling of his history.

In addition, the antebellum years were rife with the building tensions that would lead to the Civil War. In 1820, when, as Smith recounted, he was visited by "God the Father and His son Jesus Christ," crisis was in the air.

So was confusion. The religious revivals of the Great Awakening left in their wake a profusion of sects, mainstream offshoots and tropes; some families, including Smith's, ended up with a kind of grab bag of beliefs, all in a jumble. Nationally, rumbles of greater trouble to come mingled with the fallout from recurrent economic panics (including America's first major depression, in 1819).

The story of the peculiarly American religious sect founded in 1830 as the Church of Jesus Christ (of Latter-day Saints) shortly after Smith's revelations were published in *The Book Of Mormon* has been told often and more comprehensively than this book has room to discuss. What is pertinent to our story is Joseph Smith's surprisingly personal connection to Salem and the residual influence of the religion he founded, which, for a short time, blossomed in nineteenth-century Salem.

According to his mother's account of his life[59] (a book with a very complicated publication history), Joseph Smith, as a child, traveled to stay "with his uncle, Jesse Smith, to Salem, for the benefit of his health, hoping the sea-breezes would be of service to him, and in this he was not disappointed." The six-year-old boy was recuperating from surgery on his leg, in which a typhus infection had settled. It is not clear how long his visit lasted, but settled, prosperous and architecturally beautiful Salem had not seen the last of Smith.

As a young man, Smith became well known in his native region of Palmyra Township, New York, as one who employed "seer stones"[60] and mysticism in searching for actual, physical, buried treasure. Apparently, at least once, he ran into some legal troubles pursuing this activity. Treasure seeking and divining (as in folk magic) are elements that consistently appear in accounts of his life and work.

In July 1836, from their settlement at Kirtland, Ohio, Smith and other leaders of the church—Hyrum Smith (1800–1844), Sidney Rigdon (1793–1876) and Oliver Cowdery (1806–1850)—began a missionary trek toward Salem, arriving in late August. Later, they were joined by Brigham Young (1801–1877) and Lyman E. Johnson (1811–1856), other Latter-day Saints (LDS) leaders.

The catalyst for the journey to Salem varies, depending on whose accounts you read. The LDS church was facing serious financial stress. On a personal level, Smith had become a father yet again, his wife, Emma, giving birth on July 20, 1836, to a son.

While in Salem, Smith reported receiving a timely revelation:

> *A revelation*
> *Salem (Mss.) August 6, 1836.*
> *I the Lord your God am not displeased with your coming this Journey, notwithstandig* [sic] *your follies. I have much treasure in this city for you, for the benefit of Zion; and many people in this city, whom I will gather out in due time for the benefit of Zion, through your instrumentality: Therefore it is expedient that you should form acquaintance with men in this city, as you shall be lead, and as it shall be be given you. And it shall come to pass, in due time, that I will give this city into your hands, that you shall have power over it, insomuch that they shall not discover your secret…parts; and its wealth, pertaining to gold and silver, shall be yours. Concern not yourselves about your debts, for I will give you power to pay them…And inquire…diligently concerning the more ancient inhabitants and founders of this city, for there are more treasures than one for you in this city…*[61]

Those who do not adhere to the narrative of a religious purpose for the Salem adventure point to an article in Ohio's *Painesville Telegraph*. The article claimed Salem contained buried (possibly pirate) loot. This starkly earthly motive was, by secular accounts, the true main focus of the journey. Joseph, of seer-stone fame, was simply plying his old trade of treasure hunting.

In the online account detailing the adventure, "Doctrine and Covenants and Church History Seminary Student Study Guide—Treasure in Salem," Mormons also lay the episode solidly at the door of one William Burgess, who "claimed to know where a large amount of money was available in Salem, Massachusetts." According to this account, Smith and the others trustingly went to Salem to meet Burgess, who then couldn't remember where the money was.[62]

Richard Lyman Bushman, in his book *Joseph Smith: Rough Stone Rolling*, says that the group nevertheless persisted in looking for the treasure:

> *For two weeks, the men taught from house to house, taking time out to visit the famous East India Marine Society museum like ordinary tourists. On August 20, Rigdon lectured on "Christianity" at the lyceum. All the while they looked for the treasure-house. On August 19, Joseph wrote Emma that "we have found the house since Bro. Burgess left us, very luckily and providentially, as we had one spell been most discouraged." They were plotting how to get possession. "The house is occupied, and it will require much care and patience to rent or buy it." Joseph said they were willing to wait months if necessary, but by September, the party was back in Kirtland with no treasure for their pains.*[63]

Nevertheless, Salem was to provide more "saints" to the fold. Native Salemite Benjamin Ashby (1828–1907) left a fairly plain and straightforward account of his family's conversion to Mormonism:

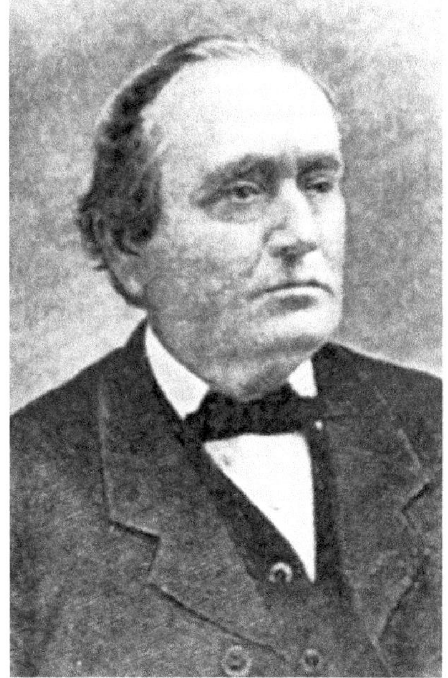

Erastus Snow, whose Mormon missionary work in Salem bore fruit for the church.

> *In the year 1839 or 1840 there came to Salem, Erastus Snow, preaching the gospel in its purity, as revealed to Joseph Smith. My father was not a member of any denomination but attended the Universalist Church of which my mother was a member because as I have often heard her say they preached the love of God for his children in contrast to the doctrines of the Orthodox churches that held to the everlasting punishment of all who did not embrace their peculiar dogmas.*
>
> *Father returned home one Sunday noon, saying he had been to hear a new religion preached by a Mormon*

in the Masonic Hall...My mind soon became enlightened upon the plan of salvation...

Mother...attended the meetings in the Masonic Hall and became convinced of the truth of the gospel. One Sunday morning father gave me some money and told me to go to Sexton and give up his pew and shortly after, he and mother were baptized into the church and though they had bore excellent characters all their days they were called crazy, and derided by relatives and friends.

We all continued to attend the meetings of the Saints and a large branch was organized...

Brother Snow who had been living in one of father's houses returned to Nauvoo and contracted for a house to be built and upon his return to Salem sold to father the lot adjoining his...

We left Salem the 14th of October [1843]...[64]

An important Salem convert to Mormonism during these early years was Nathaniel Henry Felt (1816–1887). Reverend Joseph Barlow Felt (1789–1869), whose *Annals of Salem* is a standard Salem historical source, was Nathaniel's first cousin.[65] According to a Felt family website, he was a descendant of the first accused witch executed in Salem in 1692, Bridget Bishop,[66] and was also related to Nathaniel Silsbee and Timothy Pickering. His house still stands in Salem, marked with a commemorative plaque.

Nathaniel, with his brother, was the proprietor of an Essex Street tailoring service. He converted to Mormonism in 1843 and, "with 120 new converts, began a small branch of the Church in Salem. Because of Nathaniel's position as branch president, this house became an important Mormon meeting place."

LDS leader Brigham Young sent his teenage daughter Vilate to the Felt abode the following year to continue her education. Young came to Salem several times, and it was in Salem that Young received news of Smith's assassination in Illinois in June 1844. The following year, Salem Mormons, including the Felt family and Vilate Young, left the City Named for Peace for a journey that would finally end in Salt Lake City.

There, Nathaniel embarked on a public career "that included service as Salt Lake City alderman and Utah Territorial representative." According to the Felt family website, Nathaniel married three wives under the Mormon doctrine of polygamy.

Mormons believed that revelation was not confined to the early Christian church but was continuing in contemporaneous America. Significantly, by

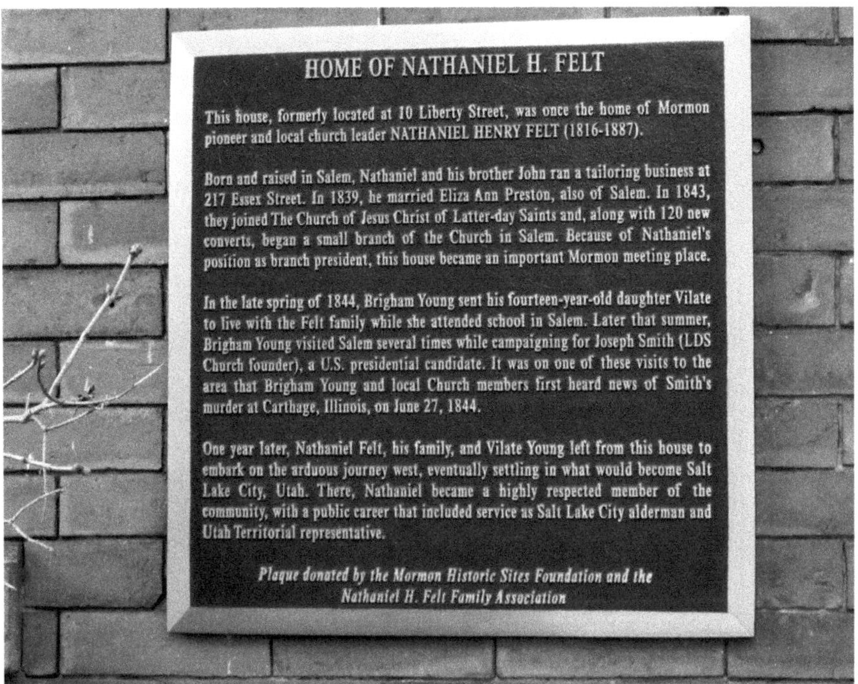

Nathaniel Felt was a Salemite who became a prominent Mormon.

the early 1850s, however, church authorities instructed that only revelations received within the Mormon faith were to be accepted as true.[67]

Spiritualists believed, similarly, that the modern age was one of unprecedented enlightenment and new understanding, shining light where older religious systems had often spread darkness. Belief in the gift of tongues (or writing in unknown foreign languages), prophecy (most often as conveyed from spiritual guides or angels), new revelations, visions and divinations and unusual healing powers were common to both sects.

Belief in the endurance of a person's unique human personality after death, its existence in the "spirit world" and the ability of the living to communicate with the dead (including apparitions, at least for the first generation of Mormons) constituted more similarities between the two and revealed their common debt to Swedenborgianism.

Mormonism, as well as Spiritualism, advocated alternative views about sexuality and what constituted divinely legitimate marriage, albeit in distinctively different ways.

As they solidified their organization (and especially after some Mormons became Spiritualists), Mormons would reject Spiritualism as "counterfeit religion" emanating from the devil, but Spiritualists took a more liberal view. Spiritualists reasoned that Mormons probably did not understand their revelatory experiences as being truly spiritualist in nature.

Salem: Symbol of Intolerance, Fanaticism and Superstition

The collective memory of that dreadful year in colonial Salem when so many were imprisoned (some never to emerge alive) and twenty innocent people were legally tortured and murdered at the hands of their neighbors has had, ever since, formative influence on Salem's development and self-image.

Salem's tarnished reputation due to the witchcraft trials was a source of sorrow, embarrassment and shame for most of the leading lights in nineteenth-century Salem. In countless venues—in every corner of the world, in print, from the pulpit, in common parlance—when superstition or fanaticism was decried or described, or a persecution of any type was reported, the name "Salem" was used as shorthand for such dark impulses.

The White murder trials in 1830 didn't help matters: the afterimage of thousands of witnesses in Salem watching the subsequent executions, not to mention the bloody violence of the crime itself, was all too reminiscent of 1692.

During the nineteenth century, despite attempts of town leaders to promote monikers such as "The Puritan City," Salem was universally and commonly called "The Witch-City" or "City of Witches." The names were far from complimentary.

This baffled and frustrated nineteenth-century Salemites. It truly rankled those who had such particular and pronounced pride in its religious heritage, intellectual and cultural accomplishments, civic and political luminaries and history of global maritime commerce, all of which, they felt, should have been more worthy of remembrance.

Throughout the nineteenth century, this unease grew ever more intense. In the buildup to, as well as during, the Civil War, Southerners mocked their Northern brethren as breeders of fanaticism and intolerance, again using Salem as shorthand in their discussions. Resentment was exacerbated by such mockery.

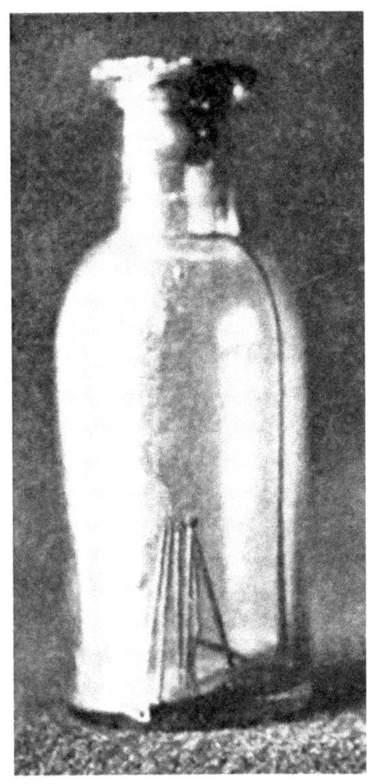

Court clerks routinely showed Salem visitors the "witch pins," with which the accused were presumably tortured in 1692.

Scholarly and popular attempts to explain the witchcraft trials began early, yet the associations of Salem with witchcraft intensified through the century to assume the shape of a crisis in leading Salem citizens' minds by the second half of the nineteenth century.

As Spiritualism gathered force, with thousands of national and international enthusiasts, and as it sparked its own controversies, "Salem Witchcraft" was reflexively mentioned as an antecedent or as an equivalent to Spiritualism by supporters and opponents alike. The equation, particularly from the pulpit, of Spiritualism with evil, demonology and witchcraft, most often with an implied reference to Salem, added to the alarm.

One of the best-known efforts to place Salem's witchcraft ordeals in context and thus to repair the town's reputation resulted from the work of the Reverend Charles Wentworth Upham. His publications, though originally issued in a limited run, became the standard references on the subject, exerting inescapable influence on historians who tackled the subject ever after.

As Upham's conclusions (which were not without controversy, especially in his treatment of Cotton Mather and other clergy) entered the popular consciousness, that influence grew even wider and stronger; indeed, it would not be until the twentieth century that historians would produce a work on Salem's witchcraft episode that would challenge Upham's primacy on the subject.

Charles Wentworth Upham and "Salem Witchcraft"

In his *Historical Sketch of the Salem Lyceum*, published in 1879, Henry Kemble Oliver wrote:

> *Mr. Upham's lectures, in 1831, on that obscure delusion, the Salem Witchcraft...became the foundation of his exhaustive work on that strange and most unhappy delusion... When delivered here, the several lectures were of great length, yet local interest in the subject, local allusions, and local names and celebrities, and the eminent fitness of treating this special theme near the place of the occurrences, excited a vivid interest, and kept the large audiences in close attention for more than two hours on each evening...*

Charles Wentworth Upham was born in St. John, New Brunswick, in 1802 (d. 1875). After graduating from Harvard in 1821, he settled in Salem. For the next twenty years, he was minister of the First Congregational Church. In 1826, he married Ann Susan Holmes (1804–1877), daughter of Abiel Holmes (1763–1837) and sister to Oliver Wendell Holmes Sr. (1809–1894).

After resigning from his ministerial post (apparently in the wake of some kind of vocal cord dysfunction due to a bronchial illness; he is described as having lost his "vocal power" and as "struggling" with the "affection" for two or three years[68]), he turned to public service and plunged more fully into indulging his longstanding love of history and writing. As was common among most of his peers, Upham produced many works during his life—besides his research on the Salem witchcraft trials.

The histories originated, as indicated in Oliver's description above, as well-received lectures before the Salem Lyceum, published in 1831 and 1832. Afterward, he continued his research, republishing enlarged and revised editions in two volumes after the Civil War. Two sons assisted in this work.

Upham actively served in many trusted civic capacities. He was a member of the Thirty-third Congress; a representative to the General Court in 1840, 1859 and 1860; and state senator in 1850, 1857 and 1858. He served as Salem's mayor in 1852. Famously, Upham became somewhat of a nemesis to Nathaniel Hawthorne, not to mention the religious mystic Jones Very, who was sent to a mental institution through the efforts of Upham and fellow ministers.

Despite this seemingly conventional and socially secure existence, Upham knew what it was like to be an "outsider," which perhaps contributed to the sympathy he showed toward the accused and the executed in his accounts of the trials. His memoirist, the Reverence George Edward Ellis, felt that Upham's writing about Massachusetts Loyalists during the American Revolution was sympathetically inclined, since he was the "son of an exiled and proscribed Loyalist" himself (Joshua Upham, his father, left for New Brunswick as a refugee during the Revolution when his estates were confiscated in 1778). As a "foreign-born" American, when the Know-Nothing party rose to power in mid-century, Upham needed to defend himself eloquently and forcefully when it was intimated that, being foreign-born, he had no right to represent Massachusetts.

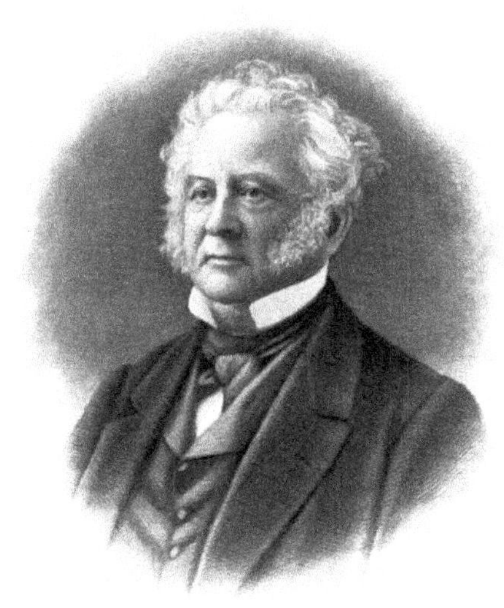

Charles Wentworth Upham

Upham's works are interesting to compare between 1831, when his first lectures on the subject were given at the Salem Lyceum, and 1867, when his *Salem Witchcraft: With an Account of Salem Village, and History of Opinions on Witchcraft and Kindred Subjects* was published. In the earlier form of the work, Upham alluded to mesmerism when discussing such things as the evidence for "ocular fascination" during the trials and made some intriguing connections between practices associated with animal magnetism and the attributes that identified a witch to earlier generations.

> *It was thought that an invisible and impalpable fluid, darted from the eye of the witch, and penetrated the brain of the bewitched. By bringing the witch so near that she could touch the afflicted persons with her hand, the malignant fluid was attracted back into the hand…It is singular to notice the curious resemblance between this opinion, the joint product of superstition and imposture, and the results to which modern science has led us in the discoveries of galvanism and animal electricity.*[69]

In the later 1867 work, he overtly equated "Modern Spiritualism" with the activities of the accusatory girls and other participants in the witchcraft "delusion," not only commenting on the historical record, but also speaking directly of the modern movement. In the intervening years, of course, Spiritualism had risen to national notoriety.

While striving to express himself in a balanced, open-minded way, Upham expressed disbelief in the claims of Spiritualists (or anyone else) who were dabbling in what he saw as supernatural practices. His basic attitude was that the accusers in 1692 were fraudulent, wicked girls.

Upham was candid about his motivations for giving the lectures and writing the books, besides the natural interest he had in historical work and his frustration that no comprehensive history had previously been done. By dint of methodical delineation of the historical context of the Salem trials, and exhaustive chronicling of activities labeled "witchcraft" through the ages and in various cultures, he wished to redeem the reputation of Salem's ancestral heritage from the "sneers" and "taunts" which so tarnished "the reputation of our home…the memory of our fathers…and…the most precious part of the inheritance of our children."

"Persons living at a distance," he said, "…treat the Salem-witchcraft transaction in the spirit of lightsome ridicule, and to make it the subject of jeers and jokes. Not so to those who have lived on, or near, the fatal scene." Awe, sorrow and shunning the "mention, and even the remembrance, of its details," said he, was the attitude of Salem's citizens ever since.

The thrust of his thesis on the subject was to show that witchcraft belief and/or practice wasn't just a Salem phenomenon, but that what happened in 1692–93 in Salem was a sorry accident of time and place, and the town bore too heavy a burden of condemnation in the eyes of the world.

Lasting as the trauma continued to be in the minds of Salemites, this made open discussion of (or dabbling in) the supernatural in nineteenth century Salem a challenging proposition. Toward the end of his 1867 book, Upham wrote:

> *Great difficulty has been experienced in drawing the story out in its true chronological sequence. The effect produced upon the public mind, when it became convinced that the proceedings had been wrong, and innocent blood shed, was a universal disposition to bury the recollection of the whole transaction in silence, and, if possible, oblivion. This led to a suppression and destruction of the ordinary materials of history. Papers were abstracted from the files, documents in private hands were committed to the flames, and a chasm left in the records of churches and public bodies…*
>
> *A subject on which men avoided to speak soon died out of knowledge. The localities of many very interesting incidents cannot be identified.*

> *This is very observable, and peculiarly remarkable as to places in the now City of Salem…In a community of uncommon intelligence, composed, to a greater degree perhaps than almost any other, of families that have been here from the first, very inquisitive for knowledge, and always imbued with the historical spirit, it is truly surprising how little has been borne down, by speech and memory, in the form of anecdote, personal traits, or local incidents, of this most extraordinary and wonderful occurrence of such world-wide celebrity. Almost all that we know is gleaned from the offices of the Registry of Deeds and Wills…*

In a footnote, he reiterates how little knowledge or discussion there still was in the Salem of his own day:

> *The reader may judge of my surprise in now discovering, that, while writing the "Lectures on Witchcraft," I was owning and occupying a part of the estate of Bridget Bishop, if not actually living in her house…while delivering those lectures in the Lyceum Hall, that we were assembled on the site of her orchard, the scene of the preternatural and diabolical feats charged upon her by the testimony of Louder and others…Tradition was stifled by horror and shame. What all desired to forget was forgotten. The only recourse was in oblivion; and all, sufferers and actors alike, found shelter under it.*[70]

Returning to February 1892, Academy Hall, 200th Anniversary of the "Witch" Trials

Barrett Wendell (1855–1921) was known to the three generations of students who took his classes at Harvard as a generous, genial and passionate scholar who was, in the opinion of his fellow Academy of Arts and Sciences colleague Robert Grant, "a positive constructive force in the fields of English composition and of comparative literature."

Yet as famous as he was for his writings and his groundbreaking restructuring of the "Literary History of America," Wendell was equally celebrated for his personal characteristics; he was, as Grant felicitously put it, "a man of pronounced individuality, warm in his sympathies…free from littleness…" and, Grant strongly implied, rather eccentric, "whimsical" in his "peculiarities."[71]

As Mayor Rantoul turned the floor over to Wendell, all expected a literate and thorough treatment of the trials. All knew him to be a respected scholar, although he disclaimed specific scientific or historical learning that might allow him to adequately analyze the history of Salem witchcraft. Yet, he "suggested that his observation of modern occultism revealed to many points of likeness to matters testified in the trials of the Salem witches" and that his conclusion was that the events represented "really something resembling an epidemic of hypnotism."

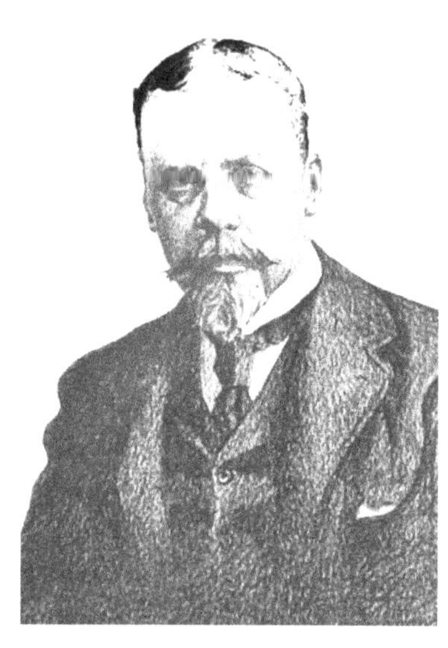

Barrett Wendell, circa 1901.

He referred to "Mr. Upham's admirable books" and had, of course, written his own studies of Cotton Mather (finding Mather less a villain than others). He had, he said, studied mediums of the present day and found them to be "fraudulent"—albeit, perhaps, self-delusional to the extent of self-hypnotizing—just as the accusing girls had been two hundred years before.

But what he said next quite possibly electrified his audience. "My own occult experiences had induced in me a state of mind that led to some speculative conclusions widely different from those commonly accepted…I am disposed to believe…that there is perhaps reason to surmise that not all the victims of the witch trials were innocent."

Professor Wendell then described his own explorations of psychic activity. His research included studying "materialized spirits," visiting trance mediums and experiments with automatic writing. The materializations took place in darkened rooms, where, in the "dim light, a small company, mostly ardent believers, were wrought up into such emotional excitement as could be awakened by hymn tunes…presently uncanny shapes began to flit about…You could not see how the trick was done, but the trick was essentially like what any number of travelling magicians perform. Before long, however, you remarked that the habitual frequenters of these unedifying exercises seemed fervently to believe in them."

However, Wendell was unsure that the mediums themselves were completely fraudulent; he suspected that, subjectively, they may have convinced themselves of the truth of their abilities. He said that the sessions always left him with a sense of "debasement."

He visited a trance medium, "a woman of high respectability, and of great apparent sincerity of character," who, he said, when in trance apparently had no knowledge of whatever might have transpired during a session. His impressions, after watching her behavior during sessions as well as afterward, when the controlling spirit left her, was that she was "an honest person, in a very abnormal state, honestly self-deceived."

Finally, he told his audience, he had experimented with automatic writing, allowing "spirits" to guide his hand. After describing the variety of materials he produced and under what conditions, he said, "The thing is not all fraud,—there is something very queer about it…" but found himself "a completely untrustworthy witness" of his own productions and reported feeling irritable, nervous and "demoralized" afterward.

In short, he said, even the slightest foray into occultism had left him, a trustworthy and honest person, morally debased and disordered in his thinking.

As he discussed the similarities to 1692 in the activities "of our own time" ("how curiously some…educated minds…are recurring to kinds of mysticism that have so long seemed purely superstitious…we see these honest, intelligent mystics all about us"), Wendell speculated there were, truly, some ancestral, vestigial "powers of perception" operating in "the remote psychologic past of our race." Perhaps hypnotism (mesmerism) tapped into this perceptive ability.

The professor pointed out that Puritan culture was steeped in mystical contemplation of (and fearful insecurity about) the will of God and personal salvation, a preoccupation that permeated all aspects of daily life. Puritan culture was closer, he ventured, to vestigial powers of perception, which modern life neither required nor stimulated—except in "abnormal" circumstances.

Wendell speculated that "the bewitched sufferers at Salem often hypnotized themselves," and that, furthermore, the teenage, suggestible, "bewitched" girls had initially been hypnotized by others. Wendell opined records of the trials suggested "among those who first dragged the wretched girls down may have been some of the accused."

Certainly there was evidence that early Salemites, like others of their time, observed "white magic" customs. Wendell said he believed that a future researcher might confirm that some of those laboring under the "iron creed" of Calvinism, which "forbade all hope of salvation to any but the elect of a capricious God," had, "in a moment of despair," dabbled in the occult, experimenting with ways to divine the judgment of God or the future of their souls. The resulting "mysterious phenomena" was interpreted as the "direct handiwork of God or Satan."

During such experiments, hypnotic excesses ran rampant, and since even dabbling in the occult could be "morally debasing," as he had outlined carefully in his talk, perhaps, just perhaps, the temptation to continue exercising such power over others resulted in the terrible backlash of the "witch hysteria." The picture he drew—hypnotic subjects, later hypnotizing themselves, fixating on the accused, with "spectral" manifestations part of the entire trance experience—must have resonated with his audience, now long accustomed to accounts of mesmerized subjects and their strange behaviors, reading daily accounts of séances and ads for magnetic healers.

The speaker who took the floor after Wendell, the Reverend Charles B. Rice of Danvers, apparently most emphatically demurred with the good professor's conclusions. Reverend Rice, introduced as the successor to Samuel Parris, said he had come down especially to see that not all the sin of the trials was heaped upon Danvers, where, of course, the trouble first erupted, and although he agreed that "the afflicted girls were possessed of a hypnotic hysteria, mixed with wickedness," it was his opinion that each of the accused witches were guiltless.

When Professor Wendell's paper was published in the *Essex Institute Historical Collections* some months later with the title "Were the Salem Witches Guiltless?" a short paragraph was appended to the end of the text.

> *NOTE: It is interesting to reflect that if the views presented in this paper are valid, the witch trials, far from being abortive, may have accomplished a result of lasting importance in the history of New England. There was no more playing with occultism here, I think, until modern Spiritualism arose, to be followed by the excessive interest in occult matters so notable within the last ten years. Is it not possible that the witch trials, surrounding the whole subject with horror, may actually have checked for more than a century the growth of a tendency which unchecked might gravely have demoralized our national character?*

Chapter 3

Spirited Conversations

DEDICATION.
TO THE WISE AND MIGHTY BEINGS THROUGH WHOSE INSTRUMENTALITY THE SPIRITUAL TELEGRAPH OF THE NINETEENTH CENTURY HAS BEEN CONSTRUCTED;

TO THE BENEFICENT AND POWERFUL SPIRITS THROUGH WHOSE SUBLIME LABORS THE IMMORTAL WORLD CAN COMMUNE WITH THE MORTAL DWELLERS OF EARTH;

THIS BRIEF, FRAGMENTARY, AND MOST IMPERFECT RECORD OF THEIR DIVINE MINISTRATION, UNDERTAKEN AT THEIR COMMAND, AND EXECUTED UNDER THEIR SUPERVISION, IS REVERENTLY AND GRATEFULLY INSCRIBED BY THEIR FAITHFUL AND DEVOTED MEDIUM,
EMMA HARDINGE.[72]

In 1869, English-born Emma Floyd Hardinge Britten, former opera singer, actress and clairvoyant medium of widespread fame, penned a massive history of the first twenty years of the spiritualist movement.[73] "Modern Spiritualism"[74] was given its nineteenth-century push by the phenomenon of the "Rochester Rappings," in which the teenage Fox sisters, Kate and Margaretta (and later, older sister Leah), demonstrated mediumistic powers by apparently communicating with spirits through a variety of rappings and knocks, usually given in response to questions put to the "spirits."

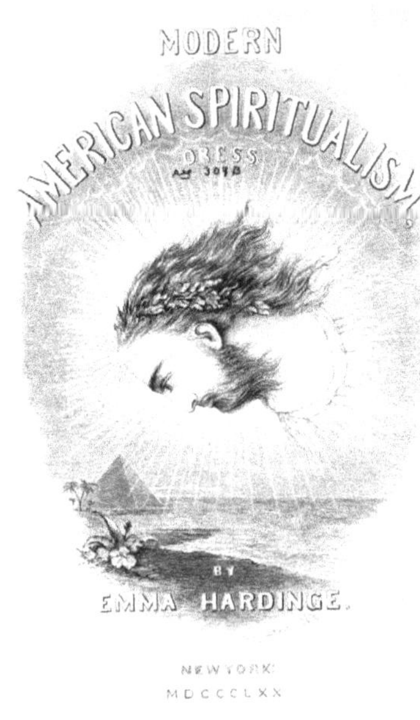

The frontispiece to Emma Hardinge Britten's history of the first twenty years of *Modern Spiritualism.*

After word got around about this "First Spiritual Telegraph on Earth," neighbors began to flock to the house to witness the mystery. When the sisters later gave public demonstrations to packed auditoriums and moved to New York City (settling in Barnum's Hotel), they were visited by some of the most famous intellectuals of the day, who either came away convinced of the veracity of spiritual communication, or, most often, at least willing to investigate further.

Among these visitors were Horace Greeley (1811–1872), who became an ardent believer and champion of the cause; novelist James Fenimore Cooper (1789–1851); George Ripley (1802–1880), a founder of Brook Farm; historian George Bancroft (1800–1891); poet William Cullen Bryant (1794–1878); and Nathaniel Parker Willis (1806–1867), bon vivant editor of the influential *Home Journal.*

One of the most important converts was Judge John Worth Edmonds (1816–1874), who served in the New York State Legislature and as president of the Senate and judge of the Supreme Court of New York. Eventually resigning his position due to the controversy raised by his belief in Spiritualism, he became a medium himself and published volumes of the communications he received. His scientific and logical approach to discussing them aroused great interest. His daughter, Laura, also became a well-known trance medium.

The judge was an important addition to the spiritualist cause since his undoubted intellect and acumen contributed to the credibility of the movement, and he is considered a major figure in the history of Spiritualism.

This put the entire controversial matter into mainstream American consciousness. The growth of religious revivalism, the breakdown of sectarian rigidity and proliferation of "new" religious experiments; public displays of magnetic healing and trance clairvoyance; the influence of Transcendentalism, Swedenborgianism, Shaker theology and the "Inner Light" of the Quakers, mesmeric fluidity linking physical and spiritual in a harmonious whole—all had prepared the ground for the sprouting of volatile seed. The writings and leadership of Andrew Jackson Davis, according to Britten, were also crucial to the intellectual and philosophical underpinnings of modern American Spiritualism. It was quite the cauldron.

Prominent believers, particularly men of high civic reputation, learning and—especially—of scientific training, proved the most valuable and sought-after exponents of the spiritualistic ethos. If such men believed, who could argue with at least exploring the possibilities?

One of the more interesting of such conversions was that of Dr. Robert Hare (1781–1858), professor of chemistry at the University of Pennsylvania, member of the American Academy of Arts and Sciences, the American Association for the Advancement of Science, the American Philosophical Society and honorary member of the Smithsonian Institution. Hare, after building a sterling reputation as the leading chemist of his age and a man who excelled in science, especially physics, investigated the claims of Spiritualism as a complete skeptic, according to his own testimony. To test the truths of Spiritualistic

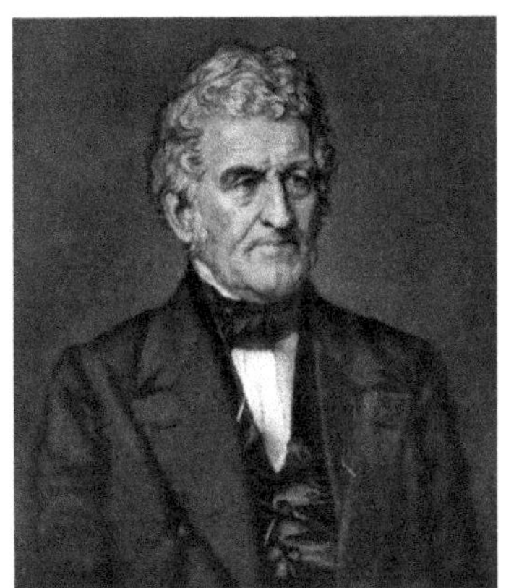

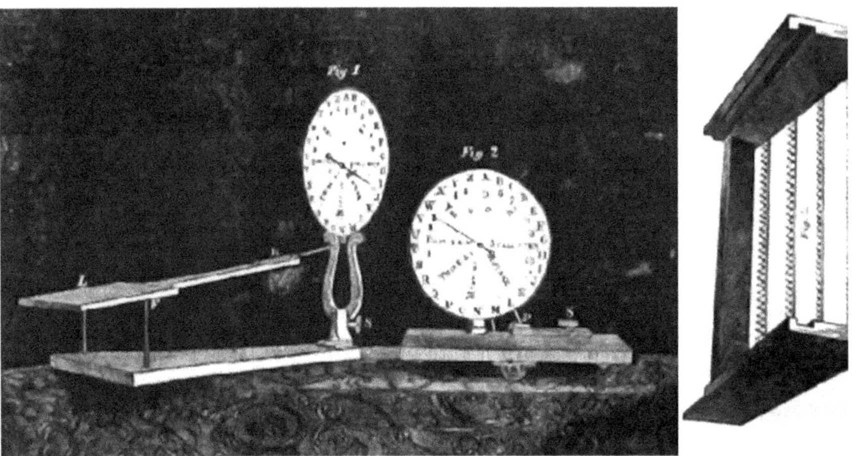

Top: Scientist-Spiritualist Robert Hare was a puzzle to his fellow scientists—and, sometimes, his fellow Spiritualists as well.

Bottom: Dr. Hare's gadget for communicating with spirits without the dangers of fraud or self-delusion on the part of the medium.

messages, he built an instrument he called the "spiritoscope" with which a sitter could bypass a medium and speak "directly with the spirits," thus eliminating the risk of fraud.

By mid-century, having become a Spiritualist himself, he was giving lectures to very large audiences, recounting his communications with spirits such as Benjamin Franklin (who seemed to be extremely busy making the rounds of Spiritualist circles). Author of a huge book on Spiritualism, Hare became one of the movement's best-known exemplars.

Mocked, humored or puzzled over by his fellow scientists, he continued in this path until his death, although, as his bio on the American Philosophical Society webpage puts it, "never an orthodox religionist, his apparent agnosticism or atheism proved as unpalatable to Spiritualists as it did to non-Spiritualists."[75]

Spiritualistic Saturation

Spiritualism permeated nineteenth-century life, growing so rapidly that, by 1869, Hardinge Britten estimated that there were eleven million Spiritualists "on the American continent" alone; her book described Spiritualist activity in each corner of the country. Accurate tabulations are difficult to document, as Spiritualists were notably averse to formal organization and creed. Estimates made by studying various publications, which proliferated rapidly and widely, concluded that perhaps nearly half the population believed in some aspect of Spiritualism.

The losses of the Civil War spurred more growth; after a slight lull, Spiritualism grew even more rapidly in the last two decades of the nineteenth century, right through the first decade or so of the twentieth. Salem itself saw the establishment of its First Spiritualist Church in 1894.[76] Through the 1890s, local Spiritualists frequently held social evenings, complete with tableaux and dancing. The Camp Progress Association of Spiritualists held picnics at their grove in Upper Swampscott; Camp Progress meetings featured a variety of mediums, many of them giving lectures.

Boston, a hotspot for Spiritualism (Philadelphia was a close rival), boasted what was one of the most important and widely circulated periodicals. The *Banner of Light*, founded in 1857, had a national audience. It published weekly lists of Spiritualist lectures and meetings, along with literary works, fairly mundane chitchat, editorials and listings of mediums and lecturers. A

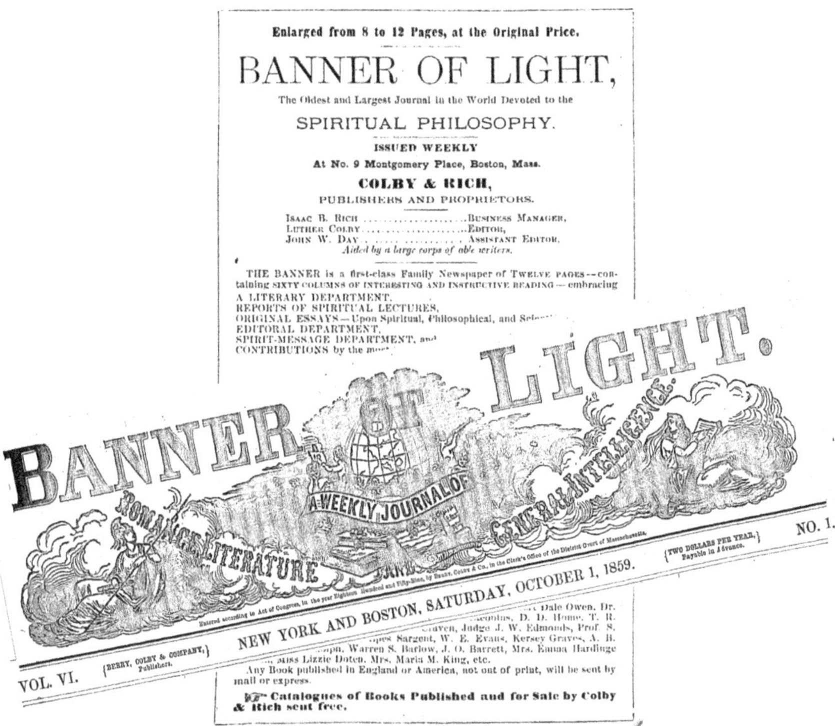

Enlarged from 8 to 12 Pages, at the Original Price.

BANNER OF LIGHT,

The Oldest and Largest Journal in the World Devoted to the

SPIRITUAL PHILOSOPHY.

ISSUED WEEKLY

At No. 9 Montgomery Place, Boston, Mass.

COLBY & RICH,

PUBLISHERS AND PROPRIETORS.

ISAAC B. RICH .... BUSINESS MANAGER,
LUTHER COLBY .... EDITOR,
JOHN W. DAY .... ASSISTANT EDITOR.

Aided by a large corps of able writers.

THE BANNER is a first-class Family Newspaper of TWELVE PAGES—containing SIXTY COLUMNS OF INTERESTING AND INSTRUCTIVE READING—embracing
A LITERARY DEPARTMENT.
REPORTS OF SPIRITUAL LECTURES,
ORIGINAL ESSAYS—Upon Spiritual, Philosophical, and Sci-
EDITORAL DEPARTMENT,
SPIRIT-MESSAGE DEPARTMENT, and
CONTRIBUTIONS by the most

Dale Owen, Dr.
D. D. Home, T. R.
Judge J. W. Edmonds, Prof. S.
Sargent, W. E. Evans, Kersey Graves, A. B.
Warren S. Barlow, J. O. Barrett, Mrs. Emma Hardinge
Miss Lizzie Doten, Mrs. Maria M. King, etc.

Any Book published in England or America, not out of print, will be sent by mail or express.

Catalogues of Books Published and for Sale by Colby & Rich sent free.

BANNER OF LIGHT.

ROMANCE, LITERATURE AND GENERAL INTELLIGENCE.

A WEEKLY JOURNAL OF

VOL. VI. {BERRY, COLBY & COMPANY, Publishers.} NEW YORK AND BOSTON, SATURDAY, OCTOBER 1, 1859. {TWO DOLLARS PER YEAR, Payable in Advance.} NO. 1.

The *Banner of Light*, a Boston newspaper with national clout.

central feature of the paper was the publishing of communiqués from the spirit world gathered from séances held in the newspaper's offices by famed medium Frances Ann Crowell (Mrs. J.H.) Conant (1831–1875).

Everywhere, it seemed, people were discovering mediumistic abilities. Mediums did not necessarily choose their calling but were "developed" by the spirits themselves. Ritualistic circles were forming for séances; published guides advocated a balance of men and women and no more than eight as the recommended composition of a circle. Circle sessions most often began with hymn singing or, alternatively, contemplative silence. Spirits frequently announced their presence with music played on floating instruments or on the piano.

Means for communication with spirits in the Summerland (a term Davis employed to describe the spirit world) multiplied. Mediums displayed talents of clairaudience and clairvoyance. Spirits, through the medium, produced automatic writing in response to sitters' questions or simply to "converse" with those present.

Séance sitters routinely experienced table-tipping (sometimes even purely social invitations would ask guests to "come for tea and table-tipping") and watched furniture skitter across the floor as proof of spirit presence. Some physical mediums, like the famous Daniel D. Home (1833–1886), levitated and floated. Artistic mediums drew or painted the spirits they saw; others spoke in unknown languages and displayed other talents they were not known otherwise to possess.

Test mediums specifically invited questions from sitters to the spirits, questions that would prove the identity of the spirit for the sitter by giving information only the sitter or investigator would know. Healing mediums gave medical diagnosis without physical examination of the patient, "seeing"

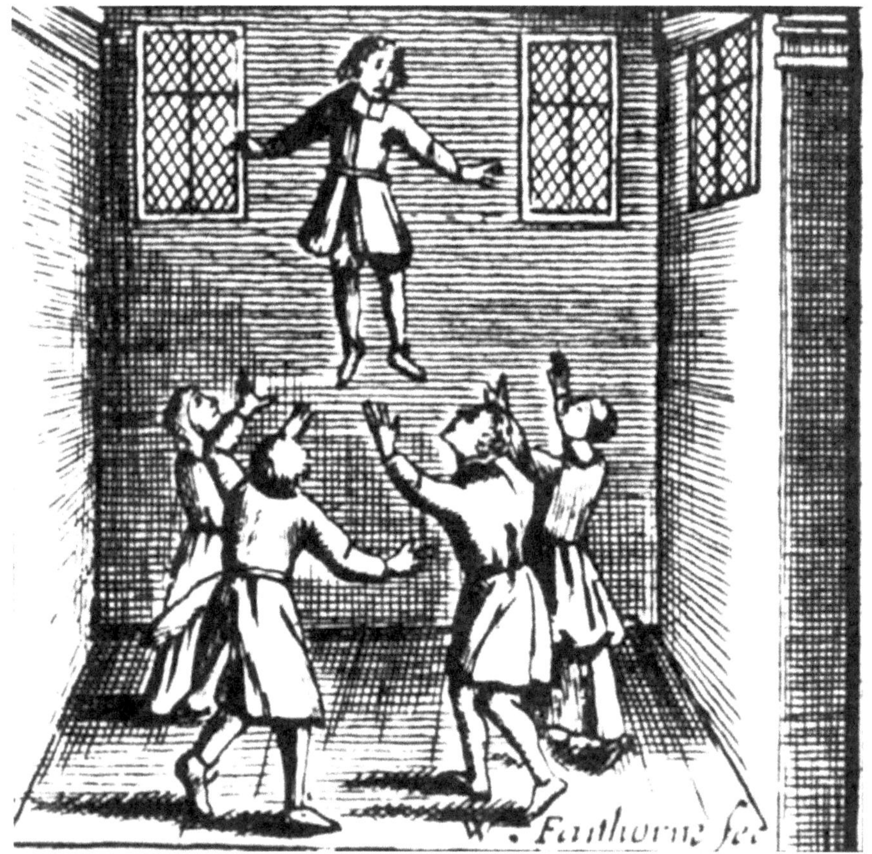

The ancient art of levitation was a common element in the demonstrations of spiritualist superstars like Daniel D. Home.

inside the subject's body. Some developed as speaking mediums, delivering messages in the voice of the departed or giving lectures publicly, but only as a conduit of the "control" spirit. There were even singing mediums.

Later in the development of Spiritualism, some séances featured "materialized" spirits; a common test session saw mediums tied and bound by sitters or investigators, then "set free" by spirits. These last developments would cause great controversy as activities all too vulnerable to fraud—as was the oddity known as "spirit photography."

Camp meetings of Spiritualists, reminiscent of evangelistic tent meetings, spread widely; regionally, Swampscott and Lynn hosted large gatherings.

Women were key to Spiritualism. Settings mattered; most often, the séance rituals were held in the domestic parlor or home, which, for nineteenth-century Americans, was not only woman's domain, but also a locus of virtue and honor. It was sacred space.

Women dominated the role of medium; those who took to the lecture circuit provided (for some areas of the country) the first example of a woman lecturer most in their audience had ever seen. The ritual of a séance gave women mediums authority and power, and the emotional context for the messages sought and received certainly would have reinforced that power with the sitters in the circle. Since not a few of those sitters carried authority in the wider world, one can readily see how the influence of women mediums extended beyond "the darkened room."

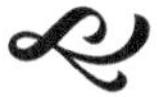

Spiritualists had no creed, no hierarchy and no organized church (until close to the turn of the century), so what did they believe?

In the preface to *Modern American Spiritualism*, Hardinge Britten declared long, deep roots to the contemporary movement (hence the designation of nineteenth-century Spiritualism as "modern"). She alluded to an idea that yet again linked Salem "witchcraft" to a metaphysical legacy:

> *The entire history of the race…ever has, and ever will be found, marked with the shadowy outline of a second world of existence, supersensuous to that of mortality…mystic writings are discovered everywhere…*
>
> *Sometimes we label them "religion," at others denounce them by the weird name of "magic," "witchcraft," or "sorcery;"…in the age when bold assertions or denial can no longer serve the cause of true philosophy,*

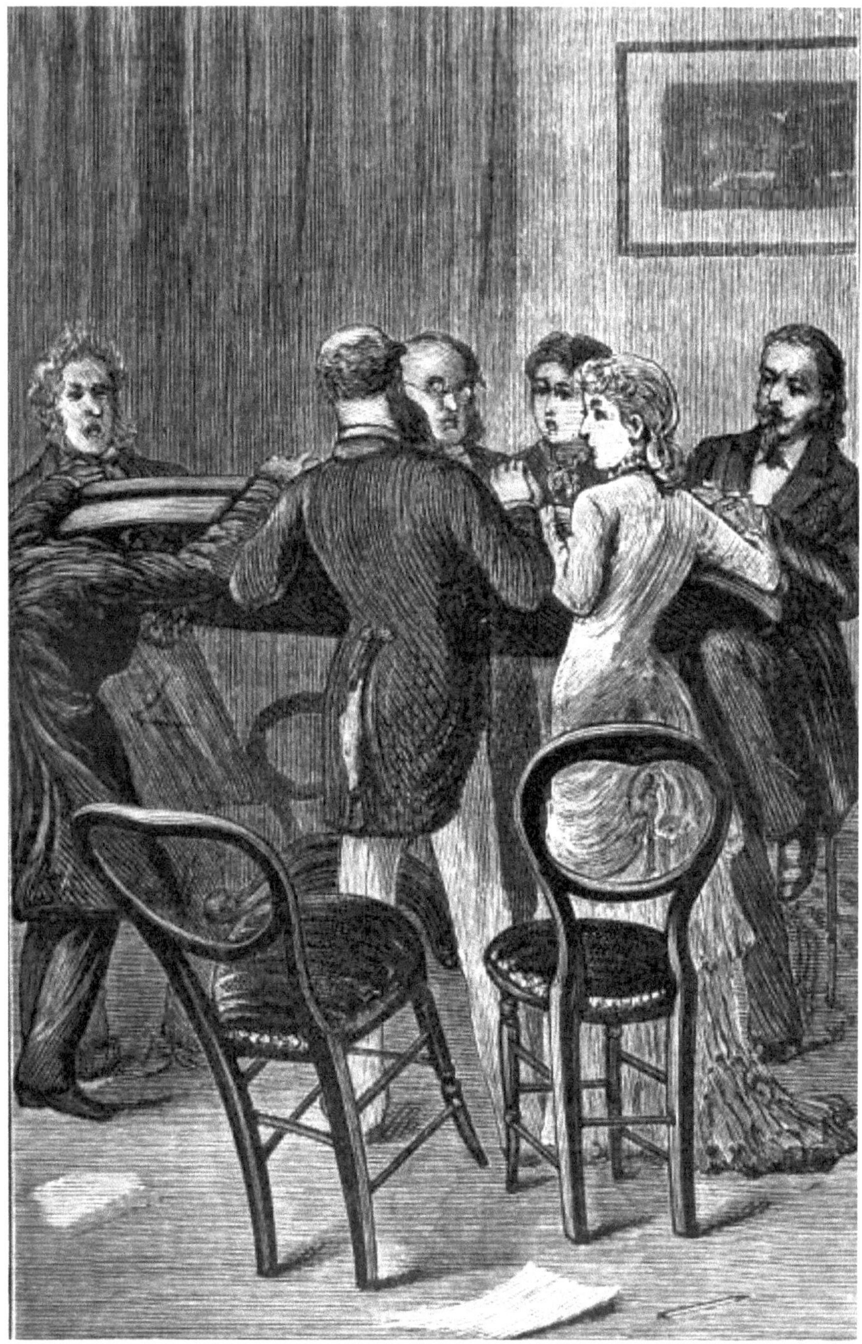

Table-tipping was a common feature of spirit communication and, sometimes, at social gatherings unrelated to sittings.

> *much less religion, comes the dawning of a day of spiritual science, in the vast and overwhelming tides of occult power that for twenty years have swept the continent of North America...*
>
> *Spiritualism, with a large majority of its American adherents, is a religion, separate in all respects from any existing sect, because it bases its affirmations purely upon the demonstrations of fact, science, and natural law, and admits of no creed or denominational boundary...its aims must encompass the whole human race in membership.*[77]

By mid-century, some defining tenets of Spiritualism had evolved:

✡ Spiritualists rejected supernaturalism and upheld the movement as resting firmly on principles of natural law;

✡ Physical manifestations of spirit and external proofs (i.e., photographs) were sought fundamentally as supportive to the scientific, progressive nature of Spiritualism;

✡ Spiritualist cosmology emphasized evolutionary and continual progress toward obtainable knowledge;

✡ Spiritualism opened the door to a higher level of spiritual development for beings both earthbound and those in the spirit, answering needs the established churches no longer could or would;

✡ Spiritualists held that the individual could have direct experience of "God," that human beings did not need to be "saved" from a fallen, sinful state; and

✡ Since upholding the rights of the individual to "own themselves" in every way was central to Spiritualism, Spiritualists were active in reform movements such as abolitionism and women's suffrage and had particular views of what constituted a true marriage.

Spiritualism was manifestly *not* about the occult, *not* secret, *not* hidden, but was open to rational evaluation and intellectual exploration—including scientific tests. Those attending séance circles hoped or expected to increase their understanding of the natural, not the supernatural, universe.

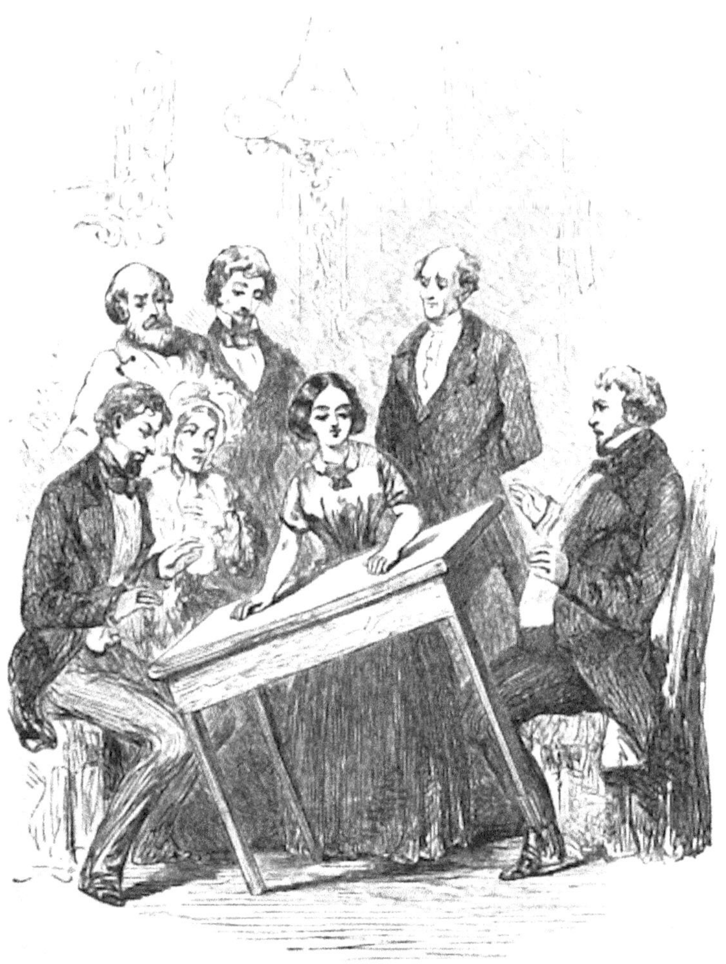

More table-tipping.

The human personality continued to progress toward its own unique state of spiritual perfection after the change from physical, earthly form to another dimension of existence. Lost children continued to grow "older" and develop toward adulthood. It follows, from this reasoning, that death represented a continuum, not a break.

Communication "with spirit" during séances or otherwise was part of the proof of this continuum. With the medium as the right "tool," conversations between the departed and those on earth were facilitated just as one would use the telegraph or telephone for earthbound communication.

In a city such as Salem, so proud of its scientific heritage, diverse in its religious life, one would expect to find an open embrace of such a movement.

However, history's labels for such explorations—just as Hardinge Britten had written, "Sometimes we label them 'religion,' at others denounce them by the weird name of 'magic,' 'witchcraft,' or 'sorcery'"—well, those labels threw a unique, shadowy challenge squarely at "The Witch City." With the last decades of the century, Salem finally began to answer the challenge in earnest.

Home-Grown Psychic: Charles Henry Foster

A few short years after Charles W. Upham gave his lectures on Salem witchcraft, a baby boy was born in the Salem household of former mariner Joshua L. Foster. Both parents would later say that seeing spirits and having visions was simply accepted family activity, a normal occurrence, and they supposed spirit communication to be common to most other families. His mother would later tell her son's biographer[78] that she had often called on her spirit friends to rock their little boy in his cradle, as the family could not afford household help when he was born.

Little Charles H. Foster (1833-1885)[79] thus was nurtured in an atmosphere conducive to his development as one of the more famous physical mediums of the century and perhaps the first true Salem psychic celebrity of the nineteenth century. A test and physical medium, he also reportedly had the abilities to levitate and to manifest psychically derived messages in blood-raised letters on his own skin. This peculiarity certainly carved his permanent niche in the spiritualist world.

During his fifty-two years on the earthly plane, his fame would spread worldwide, and he was fortunate to have a biographer, George C. Bartlett, who not only traveled with him as he gave his séances, readings and demonstrations, but who also collected newspaper articles, anecdotes, letters and other ephemera along the way. Many of these were conveniently published along with Foster's biography a few years after the psychic's passage to the "other side."

Bartlett always maintained that he was "personally…not convinced of any spirits or spirit world, believing that science will eventually explain the workings of the mind whether conscious or unconscious…whatever happens in this world comes from this world." Nevertheless, his account of Foster was sympathetic and supportive of the seer's claim to fame, and Bartlett apparently spent the rest of his life writing about and investigating psychic phenomena.

Thus we have an interesting document of the many readings, séances and even the pranks that filled Foster's career. Some of the stories are remarkable for their emotional impact. Bartlett's biography makes highly interesting reading for the student of nineteenth-century life, for through his work, Foster was acquainted with leading luminaries of the time—political figures, royalty, writers, artists and musicians—and the intersections were sometimes startling, always fascinating.

So friendly was he, for instance, with musical celebrity Louis Moreau Gottschalk (1829–1869), that he named his own son (by his second wife) Louis Gottschalk.[80] Bartlett also recounts that they spent time with Ole Bull (1810–1880) in Maine, listening to the famed violinist play well into the night. Foster loved poetry and knew Longfellow, Whitman, Winter and Arnold, among others. He reportedly was the model for the character of Margrave in *A Strange Story* by Lord Edward Bulwer Lytton.

In an August 1910 magazine article, Bartlett quoted John Ashburner, MD, member of the Royal Irish Academy, and author of *Notes and Studies in the Philosophy of Animal Magnetism and Spiritualism*, who wrote of his impressions of Foster when the seer was in London in 1863.

> *The utter simplicity of Mr. Foster's modus operandi is also in his favor. He has no paraphernalia—absolutely none. No cabinet...no dimly lighted room, no ropes, no instruments, or contrivances of any kind. The sunlight is welcome in the daytime, and the full blaze of the gas in the evening. An ordinary table, a supply of writing paper and a few pencils constitute his entire stock in trade.*[81]

Sir Arthur Conan Doyle, in his *The History of Spiritualism*, described Foster as "extravagantly dual. He was not only Dr. Jekyll and Mr. Hyde, but he represented half a dozen different Jekylls and Hydes. He was strangely gifted, and on the other hand he was woefully deficient. He was an unbalanced genius, and at times, I should say, insane."[82]

Sadly, the last years of Foster's life were, indeed, spent in illness, first of body and then, more lastingly, of mind; after hospitalization in the Danvers insane asylum, he was brought home to Salem and cared for in his aunt's house.

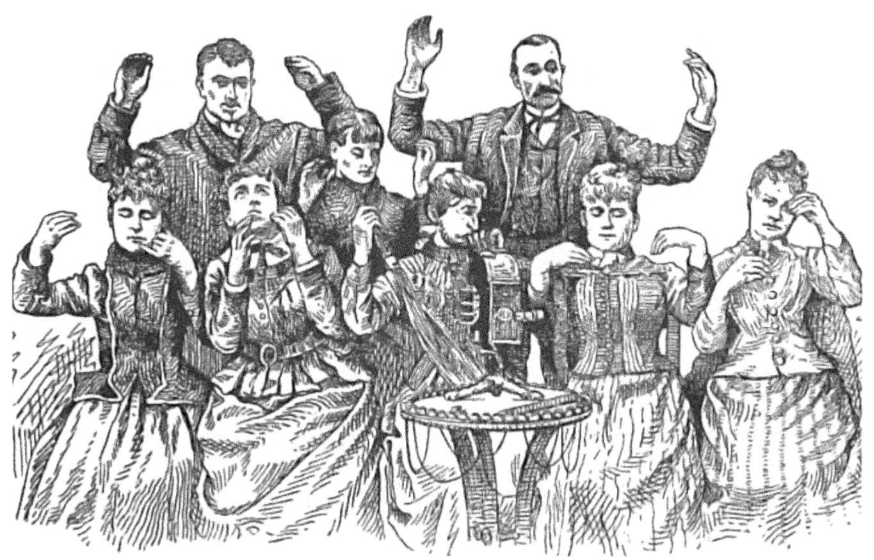

People under the influence—of just what, we leave to you to guess.

After he died, some of the friends who gathered at the house at 14 Williams Street to memorialize him were prominent in spiritualist and civic circles. Among them were Reverend Fielder Israel, a Thirty-second degree Mason and minister of Salem's First Unitarian Church from 1877 to 1889 (when, sadly, he was found dead in his study, a suicide); ex-alderman John B. Bettis; Luther Colby, founder and publisher of the *Banner of Light*; John R. Bassett; and Reverend George S. Hosmer.

Before Foster's burial in Harmony Grove Cemetery, his eulogist, the well-known Spiritualist William Juvenal Colville (1862–1917) spoke of Foster's last hours on earth as being filled with "the music of the spheres" sounding in his ears as "spirit friends, kind and wise, clustered round his bed, and welcomed him with open arms into their fairer state of being" with his "health, youth and mental vigor more than renewed."

Legacies: Allen Putnam (1802–1887)

Fall-of-the-leaf time in New England: a time when, watching the slow progress toward winter, the mind turns naturally to the mysteries of death

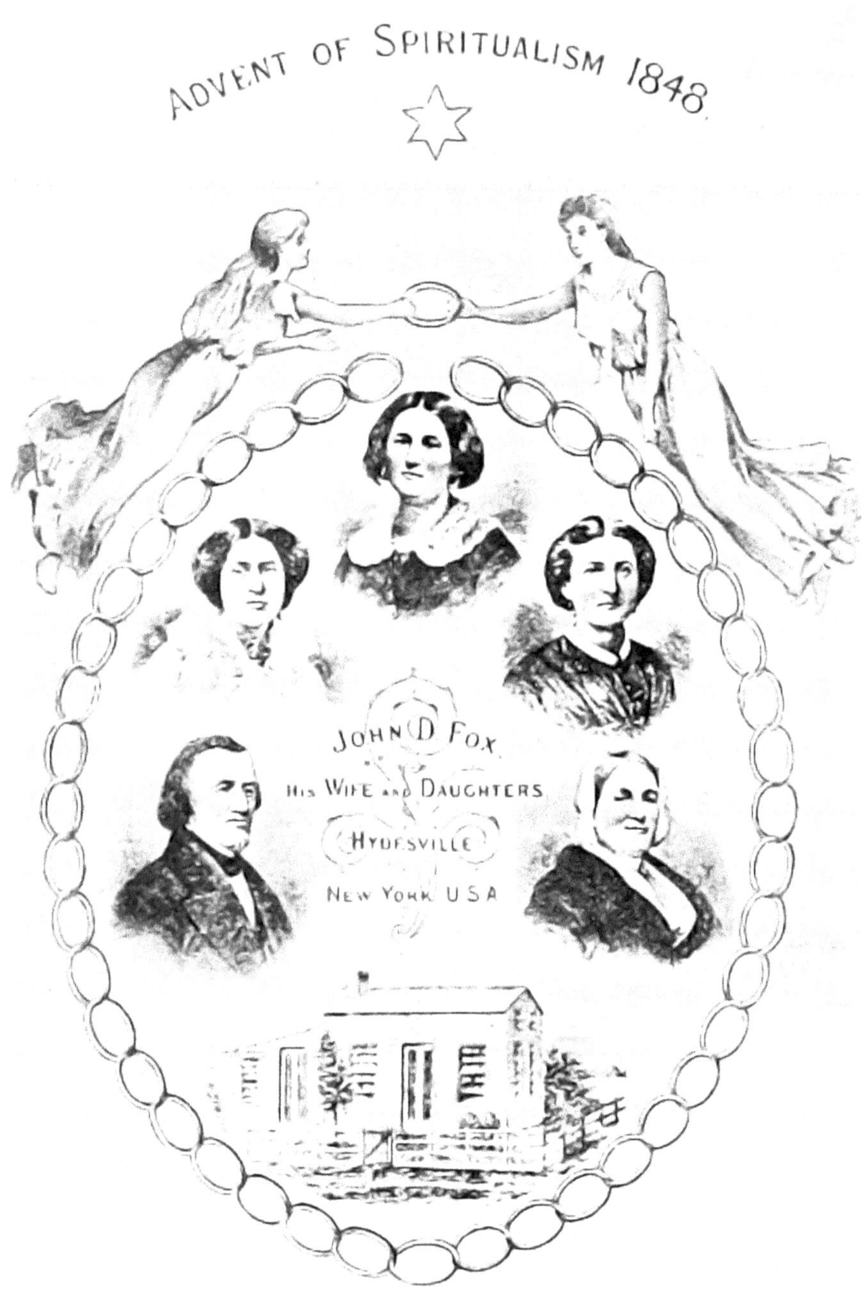

The Fox girls from Hydesville.

promising a springtime rebirth. In September 1853, a former Unitarian minister-turned-farmer-turned-businessman faced an audience of "four or five hundred" at the Roxbury, Massachusetts city hall to deliver his lecture, "Spirit works; Real but Not Miraculous."[83]

Allen Putnam, descendant of a family closely identified with the Salem witch trials, was born in Danvers and attended Harvard, graduating in 1825. After a few years as a teacher, he centered Cambridge Divinity School and became an ordained minister in 1831. He led a church in Augusta, Maine, but when his wife, Abigail (Pierce), died, his "health broke down," and he came home to Danvers, where he lived on the "paternal farm" and edited the *New England Farmer*.

In 1843, however, he married again (Hannah D. Williams) and became established in the coal business in Roxbury, a business he ran for the next twenty years. Though some of his Harvard schoolmates regarded him as a victim of "self-delusion" where Spiritualism was concerned, he was respected enough to have represented both Danvers and Roxbury in the General Court.

He married twice more during his life,[84] and though his health apparently remained a challenge to him (he described it as severe dyspepsia and complained of it often in his letters) he became not only an ardent Spiritualist during his later life, but also a prolific writer on the subject.

Amusingly, among those works, Putnam would publish *Post-Mortem Confessions: Being Letters Written Through a Mortal's Hand by Spirits Who, When in Mortal, Were Officers of Harvard College: With Comments* (Boston: Colby & Rich, 1886). On page 3, he wrote: "The chief contents of this work will consist of correspondences between its author and certain former officers of Harvard College in reference to their attack upon modern Spiritualism in 1857."

Apparently, according to this book, his Harvard colleagues experienced a change of heart along with their change to spiritual existence. All of them now knew the truth of Spiritualism, and had their "confessions"—and apologies—to make, especially about their hounding and suspension of a young divinity student, Frederick Llewellyn Hovey Willis (1830–1914), who had become a medium (and quite the cause célèbre) while attending the school.

During his Roxbury lecture, which was so well received that he was invited to give it in Boston and then beyond, Putnam gave accounts of various séances and communications from spirits that he had witnessed and received throughout his numerous explorations in Spiritualist circles.

Although he told his audience that he did not expect them to believe, and he realized that many people considered Spiritualists to be quite deluded, he felt compelled to spread the news of Spiritualism since it would not be "manly, Christian, nor pious, to deny a conviction which the facts, that my own eyes and ears were witnessing, forced upon the mind." After his résumé, he outlined the rational sensibility of belief in Spiritualism. And, far from being demonic, as some ministers were proclaiming from their pulpits, Putnam said, understanding Spiritualism fully would strengthen Christian belief.

Putnam felt it was comfort to know "that good kindred angels are present to guide our feet in the paths of truth and peace; to breathe around and through us a purer charity, a brighter hope, a serener joy, than belong to our claybound souls."

This uplifting view combined with consideration of spirit presence as a natural, not a supernatural, reality would attract many sober, sincere and utterly pragmatic minds to Spiritualism.

Joseph Gilbert Waters (1796–1878)

Perhaps the heartbreak so well known to seafaring towns such as Salem was the precipitating moment…the sad inscription after a son's name, "lost at sea." Why wouldn't a parent be tortured by the enduring mystery of just what happened, how and why?

The marriage of Eliza Greenleaf Townsend (1798–1890) and Joseph Gilbert Waters produced five sons. Joseph Linton, the eldest, worked from 1849 to 1854 at the Salem Custom House, where he would become a friend of Nathaniel Hawthorne.[85] Later, Joseph Linton worked as an employee of the Illinois Central Railroad Company. Although he remained unmarried, he became the guardian of the children of Augustus N. Dickens (brother of author Charles Dickens), with whom he worked out West. He would also assist his brother, Henry, with genealogical work.

The Waters family grew through the mid-1800s; Joseph Linton's birth was followed by Penn Townsend in March 1829; Edward Stanley, born in 1831; and the youngest, Charles Richardson, in 1835.

Music-loving, scholarly and an avid furniture collector, Henry FitzGilbert, born March 1833, would garner his greatest fame as the most talented and indefatigable genealogist of his age, with many publications to his credit. Perhaps his most famous achievement was in tracing the English ancestry of John Harvard (yes, that Harvard), documentation of which had defeated previous researchers. Only two of the brothers would marry; only one would have a child.[86]

One son, Penn Townsend, as did his revered forebears of seafaring fame and success, followed the lure of the ocean wave for his fortune. When he disappeared in 1852—presumably beneath those waves—he was only nineteen years old.

Carefully preserved writings from beyond the grave.

Joseph Gilbert Waters, son of Captain Joseph and Mary Deane Waters, read law with John Pickering and graduated from Harvard in 1816. Toward the end of his career, he served as trial-justice of the District Court of Southern Essex and, for many years, as a judge in the Salem Police Court. He also served as state senator in 1835 and was secretary of the Essex Historical Society for twenty-one years (before it was merged into the Essex Institute).

Joseph G. Waters's bride in 1825, Eliza Greenleaf Townsend, came from one of the most prominent Colonial and provincial families. When Judge Waters began his career, the White murder had just occurred. Waters acted as secretary of the Vigilance Committee, which worked on the crime and was instrumental in tracking down some of the key evidence.[87]

His fascinating biographical sketch of the Reverend William Bentley (Waters had belonged to Bentley's parish in his youth), drawn from an address he gave at the 150th anniversary of the East Church, appeared in a 1905 Essex Institute edition of the minister's published diaries. In all aspects, Waters was a well-respected man, one who made both consistent economic and civic contributions to his town and region.

Though there is no document that definitively pinpoints cause and effect, Judge Waters (and probably his wife, although, again, archival evidence is somewhat oblique) became interested in Spiritualism a few years after the loss of his son Penn Townsend and began attending séances and sittings regularly in Boston. Since Penn is simply listed as "lost at sea" in most family accounts and genealogical records, the desire to know if he was truly dead or possibly alive out there beyond the horizon may have been overwhelming. At any rate, the loss of Penn obviously had a serious impact.

The picture that emerges from reading Judge Waters's letters and other documents in the archives is one of an intelligent, thoughtful, kind and intellectually curious man who expressed himself (at least in what remains on paper) in fairly conventional, mainstream terms when it came to religion. He inspired warm feelings of friendship with all his correspondents, and he had a wide circle of acquaintances, friends and colleagues.

It was evident that he became a serious Spiritualist, and as time went by, he corresponded with some of the leading lights of the Spiritualist community. Charles H. Foster hoped Waters would "avail" himself of Foster's "medium powers for your further development" when they were back in Salem. Emma Hardinge Britten called him the "last survivor of a large and much esteemed circle of friends in Salem" in an undated letter. He was kept personally informed of proceedings during the controversy which arose at Harvard in 1857, leading to the expulsion of Frederick Willis, the young divinity student who, after developing mediumistic powers, was called to defend himself against charges of immorality and fraud before the college. Willis, whose health was jeopardized by the matter but who went on to have a busy mediumistic career, wrote at least one letter directly to Judge Waters.

Allen Putnam, who wrote frequently, helped to organize and set up circles and sittings with mediums in Boston. Writing to Waters in September 1856, he invited the judge to "a full meeting of our choice circle of six" in Boston to meet with medium "Miss Burbank," who, according to Emma Hardinge Britten, was a "trance medium of the first order, and gives evidence of superior spirit control and inspiration." Burbank, who held four circles a week, each with a particular theme or intent, seemed to have traveled between cities, for Putnam remarked that the circle would meet when she returned from Hartford.

Waters was joined in this circle by his friend and fellow Harvard graduate Judge Willard Phillips (1784–1873), who Putnam said expressed a "strong desire" to have the séance messages documented by a reporter. The two exchanged books such as Andrew Jackson Davis's *The Principles of Nature, Her Divine Revelations, and a Voice to Mankind.* The Davis book actually belonged to another colleague, lawyer Nathan T. Dow, fellow believer in Spiritualism and another frequent correspondent.

Judge Willard Phillips was a man of some renown. Suffering from poor eyesight, he nevertheless led successful careers in law and business and became an acknowledged literary and legal scholar. In 1814, he helped to found the *North American Review*, serving briefly as editor but continuing to contribute articles for several years. After publishing several works on law and insurance, in 1835, he and four associates obtained a charter from the Commonwealth of Massachusetts for the New England Mutual Life Insurance Company. In 1853, Harvard College awarded Phillips an honorary LLD (*legum doctor* or Doctor of Laws), and he was also elected a fellow of the American Academy of Arts and Science.

At least one séance seems to have been planned at Waters's house; however, most often he went to Boston. The Boston medium Waters seemed to visit most consistently was (Mrs. James B.) Helen Leeds, at 45 Carver Street.[88] In 1858, Waters received a letter from Laura Edmonds inviting him to become part of an association formed for "holding circles and having Mrs. Leeds as medium." Association dues were twenty-five dollars a year for "a certain number of members." Commending him by implication as a "true Spiritualist," Edmonds signed herself "Yours in the Truth."

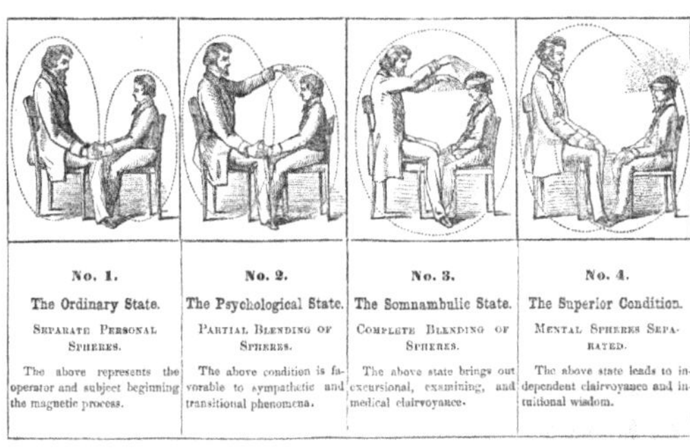

Progression from lower to higher forms of understanding.

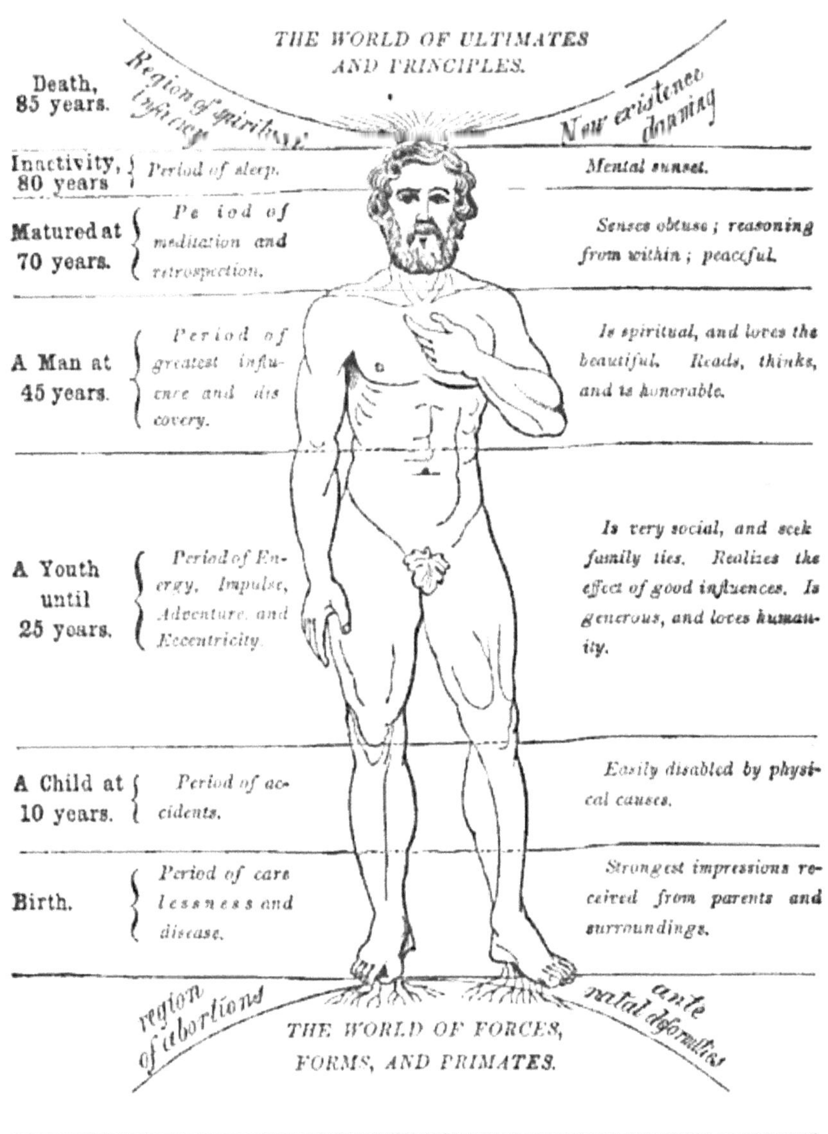

The Great Harmonia.

In a letter dated March 12, 1858, Waters received a note from Samuel C. Hart of the association informing him that Leeds's afternoon circles would start the following Monday, and in August, Waters paid the fee, thus joining the association.

Leeds was described by those who sat with her as one with "spiritual fervor, amiability, pureness of motive, and internal spiritual principle." She was, apparently, a trance and test medium; one of her spirit guides was a Native American named "Red Jacket." (Native American controls were a common feature of séances.) One sitter described physical manifestations such as floating furniture at some sessions.

Despite some health problems that seem to have tempted her to give up her mediumship and an occasional hiatus in attendance by Waters, Waters attended the Leeds circles frequently. It is not clear if Mrs. Waters attended them with her husband. There was at least one letter from Leeds to Waters that seemed to indicate warm feelings between them; she thanked him for "kind and soothing words so full of love and truth." Mediums, she said, had need of them since they had so much to contend with.

Although there is no direct indication among Judge Waters's papers as to which medium produced them, spirit communications did indeed come through from Penn; Waters carefully preserved the long, undated, ragged strips of paper with scrawled messages produced during automatic writing sessions.

A typical message from the lost son, written in messy, scrawled and ofttimes smeared pencil: "Yes dear Father God bless you It is I. your son—I wish to join dear Lydia and tell you that I too comprehend the mysterious power… Father by and by ask me say a few words to you and Mother…Penn."

One poignant message from Penn began "Darling Mother" and acknowledged her longing to "be with your boy again," yet said she should "try to be happy." Penn's short, but comforting, messages were most often accompanied by messages from a loquacious "Lydia Webb," who seemed to know Judge Waters well. Her messages are also carefully preserved along with Penn's. One message begins "Yes dear Judge what more can I say to comfort you," and in other messages, she speaks as if she and Penn had been friends on earth (or perhaps had become friends in the spirit world); he was, she said, a "beautiful boy…light and merry hearted." Lydia aspired to be a "ministering angel" to all from where she was now, which, apparently, was a beautiful and joyful state.[89]

Like Judge Edmonds, Waters and Phillips were important additions to the Spiritualist movement: that they publicly allowed their names to be

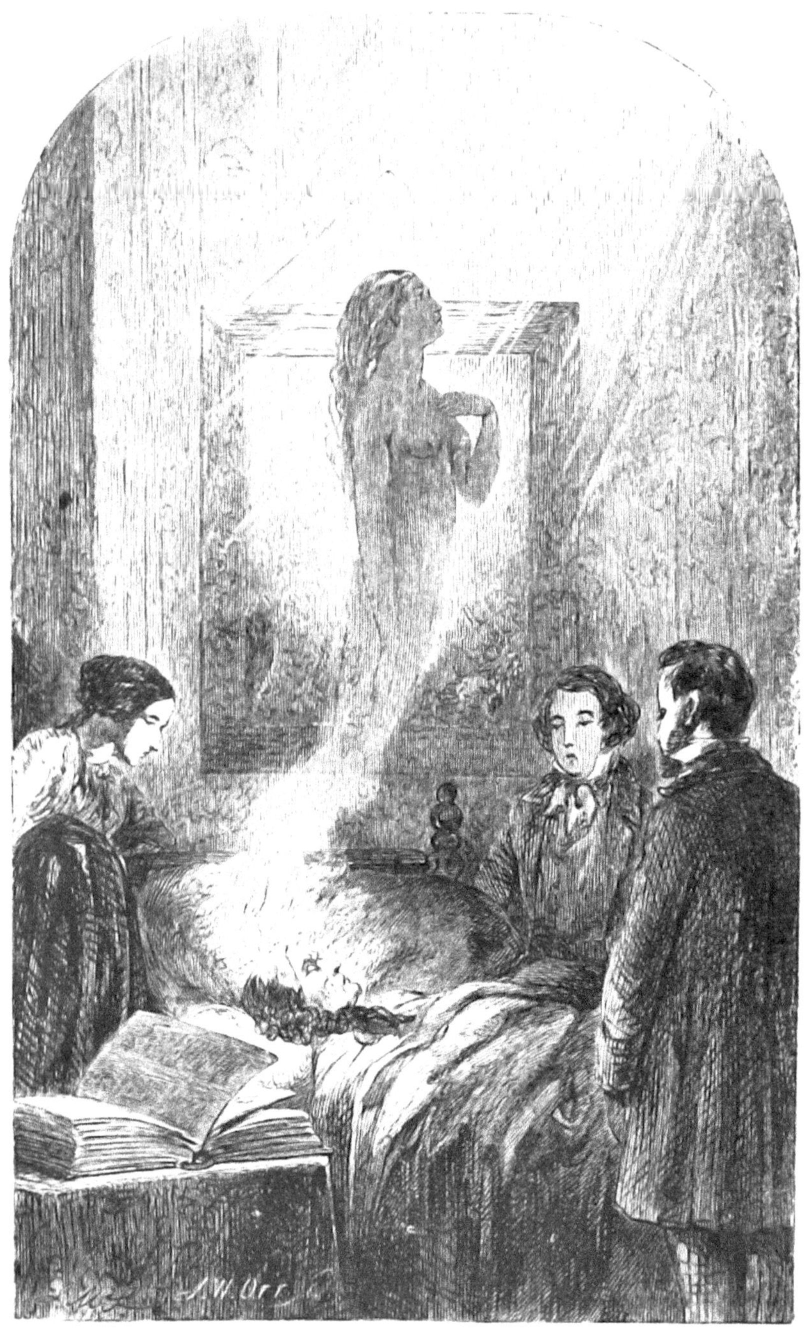

Freed from the material plane, the spirit was truly free to progress on the higher realms, filled with youthful vitality and vigor.

associated with Spiritualism helped to mitigate the criticisms of Spiritualism as a movement for crackpots and fanatics. Professional men, those with civic responsibilities and reputations for probity and rationality, were very welcome to circles for this reason.

The Hawthornes

Nathaniel Hawthorne, whose authorial talents were nurtured by and imbued with the stories and shadows of Salem's past, also married into the metaphysical. His wife, Sophia Amelia Peabody Hawthorne (1809–1871), remained deeply interested in Spiritualism and related subjects all of her life, and her sister Elizabeth (Lizzie) became an enthusiastic Spiritualist. Throughout her life, Lizzie attended séances, the results of which she confided to her sister (trying to avoid, if possible, Nathaniel's attention). Lizzie even decided at one point that Una, Nathaniel's and Sophia's eldest daughter, had mediumistic gifts—a pronouncement that did not endear her to her brother-in-law.[90] Una did display a kind of otherworldly "soul," thought her father, especially evident to him when the family lived in Italy. It seemed to worry him.

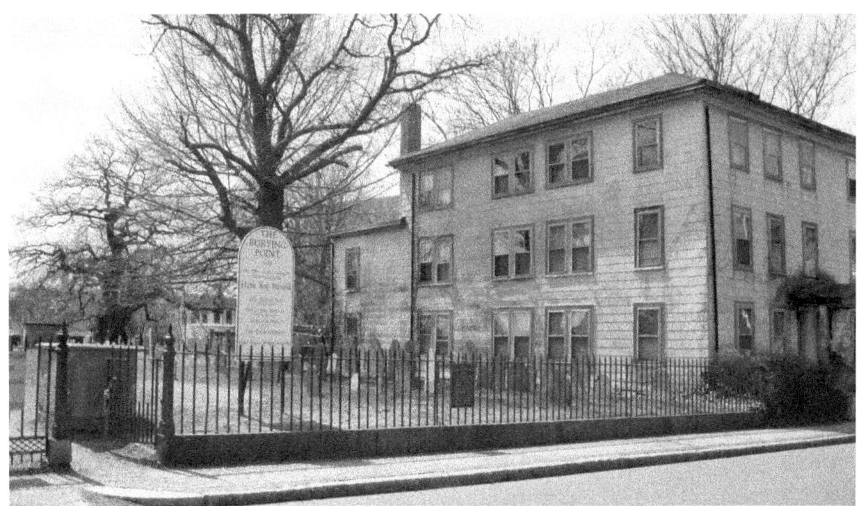

The house where Nat met Sophia.

When, during Sophia's youth, the Peabody family moved into the house on Charter Street, next to the Old Burying Point in Salem, Dr. Nathaniel Peabody, Sophia's father, had room to set up his practice. His offerings included dentistry (which in those times mostly meant extractions). Elizabeth, after translating an article detailing the work of Mesmer, became convinced of the truth of animal magnetism and felt she had a gift for it.

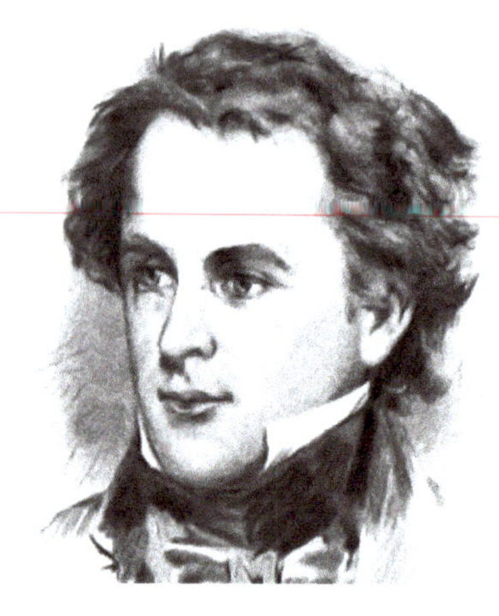
A young Nathaniel Hawthorne, handsome as the…well, you know.

Whether or not this influenced her father, he took a young dental assistant into his practice, Dr. Joseph Emerson Fiske (1811–1882), who had become more practiced in the art of magnetizing patients since we last met him conducting his early experiments. He offered to help cure Sophia of her migraine headaches with mesmeric technique. He may have treated her for a few years; when the family moved to Boston, Sophia received mesmeric treatments from others as well.

Her fiancé, Nathaniel Hawthorne, was appalled and urged her not to submit herself to the mysterious trances; he feared the power of the mesmerist in these exchanges. The sexual undercurrents of man as mesmerist, woman as subject, which was the most common configuration, also served to alarm and unsettle.

Hawthorne understood the serious physiological effects that mesmerism had and did not doubt that the clairvoyance (which seemed to be unloosed by the trance) was a powerful psychological phenomenon. He wrestled with the implications of this for years and hovered between curiosity and ambivalence most of his life.

Naturally, as most devotees of Hawthorne's works know, he used mesmerism, trance and other aspects of the metaphysical culture of his day in his short stories and books, just as he used his observations of the Shakers.[91]

Although the Hawthornes had their scattered experiences with Spiritualism throughout their lives, in England as in America, it was during the family's 1858 sojourn in Italy that they would have numerous encounters with the spirit lands. These experiences enticed Sophia further into her explorations and increased her husband's unsettled ambivalence toward séances, mediums and the entire cosmology of the movement.

The Hawthornes were invited into, and associated with, a small group of expatriate American (and English) artists living in Rome and in Florence. Spiritualism was strong among members of the group. Many of their adventures with Spiritualism began when poets Robert and Elizabeth (Barrett) Browning invited them to call.

> *June 9th.—We went last evening, at eight o'clock, to see the Brownings; and, after some search and inquiry, we found the Casa Guidi…*
> *We had some tea and some strawberries, and passed a pleasant evening. There was no very noteworthy conversation; the most interesting topic being that disagreeable and now wearisome one of spiritual communications… Mrs. Browning is a believer, and her husband an infidel.*

The Brownings had attended a séance conducted by Daniel D. Home (1833–1886), one of the most celebrated physical mediums of his day, whose special talent lay in levitations…and through whose mediumship a spirit had laid a laurel on Elizabeth's head. She was convinced of the spirit's reality. Her husband was convinced that Home had used trickery.

There was much more to come for the Hawthornes than conversation, however.

> *Last Saturday, August 28th, we went to take tea at Miss Blagden's, who has a weekly reception on that evening. We found Mr. Powers there, and by and by Mr. Boott and Mr. Trollope came in. Miss — has lately been exercising her faculties as a spiritual writing-medium; and, the conversation turning on that subject, Mr. Powers related some things that he had witnessed through the agency of Mr. Hume,[92] who had held a session or two at his house…Powers seems to put entire faith in the verity of spiritual communications, while acknowledging the difficulty of identifying spirits as being what they pretend to be. He is a Swedenborgian, and so far prepared to put faith in many of these phenomena…*

The "Miss —" was Ada Shepard, the Hawthorne children's governess, who discovered hitherto unsuspected mediumistic powers during a séance at the Villa Brichieri, where Isa Blagden (1816–1873) held her weekly literary receptions.

Hawthorne struggled with his feelings, now, more than ever, when the subject of Spiritualism was no longer just a topic of conversation but was also very much in their lives. He could not, however much he felt that "there is a mistake somewhere," ignore considerations of Spiritualist phenomena:

> *We have had written communications through Miss — with several spirits; my wife's father, mother, two brothers, and a sister, who died long ago, in infancy; a certain Mary Hall, who announces herself as the guardian spirit of Miss; and, queerest of all, a Mary Runnel, who seems to be a wandering spirit, having relations with nobody, but thrusts her finger into everybody's affairs. My wife's mother is the principal communicant; she expresses strong affection, and rejoices at the opportunity of conversing with her daughter…In the communications between my wife and her mother, I cannot help thinking that (Miss — being unconsciously in a mesmeric state) all the responses are conveyed to her fingers from my wife's mind…*

Hawthorne watched as Sophia became more immersed in the communication with her beloved mother, she finding it all "curious and wonderful." Her husband mused that it was all, somehow, a manifestation of psychology:

> *The whole matter seems to me a sort of dreaming awake. It resembles a dream, in that the whole material is, from the first, in the dreamer's mind, though concealed at various depths…the dead appear alive, as they always do in dreams…the mind speaks through the various persons of the drama, and sometimes astonishes itself with its own wit, wisdom, and eloquence, as often in dreams; but, in both cases, the intellectual manifestations are really of a very flimsy texture. Mary Runnel is the only personage who does not come evidently from dream-land; and she, I think, represents that lurking skepticism, that sense of unreality, of which we are often conscious, amid the most vivid phantasmagoria of a dream. I should be glad to believe in the genuineness of these spirits, if I could; but the above is the conclusion to which my soberest thoughts tend. There remains, of course, a great deal for which I cannot account, and I cannot sufficiently wonder at the pigheadedness both of metaphysicians and physiologists, in not accepting the phenomena, so far as to make them the subject of investigation.*
>
> *In writing the communications, Miss — holds the pencil rather loosely between her fingers; it moves rapidly, and with equal facility whether she fixes her eyes on the paper or not. The handwriting has far more freedom than her own. At the conclusion of a sentence, the pencil lays itself down… Her integrity is absolutely indubitable, and she herself totally disbelieves in the spiritual authenticity of what is communicated through her medium.*[93]

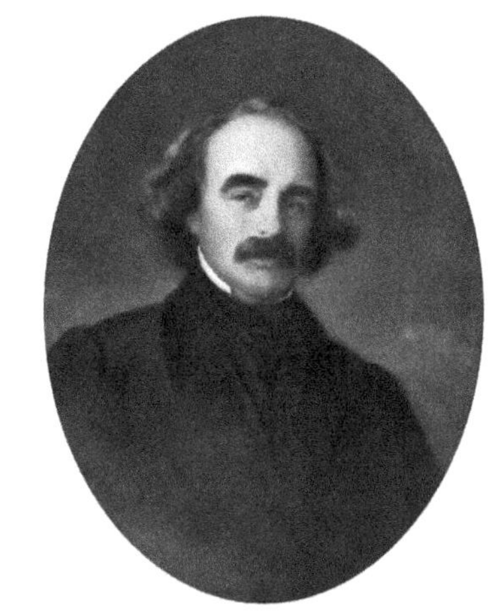

Nathaniel Hawthorne, later in life.

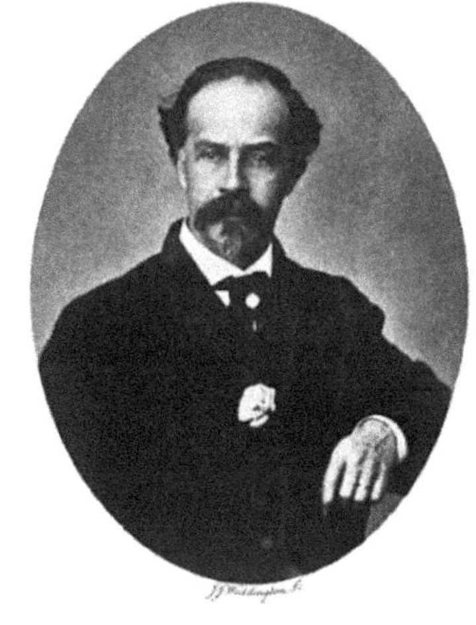

William Wetmore Story.

The Hawthornes visited often with sculptors Harriet Hosmer (1830–1908) and Hiram Powers (1805–1873), both of whom were ardent Spiritualists. They visited very frequently with fellow Salemite William Wetmore Story, now fully engaged in his art career, who was established, with his family, in the Barberini Palace in Rome. Story, too, leaned strongly toward Spiritualism.

According to art history scholar Charles Colbert, before he left for Rome, Story had joined the First Church of Humanity (Religious Union of Associationists), an organization led by William Henry Channing (1846–1854) in Boston. Story lent his studio to the meetings, and the discussions centered around "phrenology, Mesmerism and Spiritualism… He attended séances, attempted automatic writing and table turning, and mesmerized associates, all with the intent of making re-enchantment a viable stance in modern society." In his book *Conversations in a Studio*, Story gave a "measured defense" of Spiritualism, to use Colbert's words. In Italy, Story's studio continued to be a center for not only artistic but also Spiritualist discussion.[94]

It is perhaps of interest that after Nathaniel Hawthorne's death, his son Julian came into possession of "three folio volumes," the existence of which he had never before known. In his examination of the contents, he found a story of doomed romance: an "amatory correspondence between one of my own ancestors and a young lady bearing the unusual name of Mary Rondel."

Since no Mary Rondel appeared in the genealogy of the Hathorne/Hawthorne line, Julian wondered what had happened. As he probed he realized that the name "Rondel" might well have been pronounced "Runnel." He wrote to some of his Ingersoll kin, asking what they might know about the name.

They replied that, though the story was largely unknown, family tradition had passed down the story of a young Boston woman, who, in about the year 1750, had been perhaps betrothed to their ancestor Daniel Hathorne; he, however, married another. Apparently the break was abrupt, and Miss Rondel died shortly thereafter.

And that, said the sisters Ingersoll, was all they knew.

Julian wrote, "And she had ever since that time been wandering to and fro ill at ease, until this opportunity came to declare herself, and to claim the sympathy of Daniel's remote descendant. It is one of the most convincing spiritualistic stories I ever heard."[95]

Chapter 4

Psychics, Healers and Clairvoyants

Salem, just as other regional towns, just as other national cities, had a community of mediums, magnetic healers and seers. The community may have kept a lower profile in Salem than Boston, Lynn, Swampscott or Marblehead when it came to Spiritualist self-identification, but nonetheless, the great sweep of Spiritualist thought can be traced in Salem's nineteenth-century newspapers, private papers, program advertisements from various venues and, by inference, from sources outside the city. By the end of the century, clairvoyant and test mediums, as well as magnetic healers, were advertising widely and openly, even in the city directories.

Salem also received visits from some of the more famous mediums; one such luminary of the Spiritualist world was the *Banner of Light*'s Mrs. J.H. Conant, who, between 1856 and 1857, while giving public and private sessions, also "lectured in unconscious trance, each Sunday. Her addresses were principally delivered in Boston and…Charlestown, Malden, Medford, Salem, etc.—[such] as she could easily reach on Saturday afternoon, and return from on Monday without detriment to her other cares."

After appearing at the Tremont Temple in July 1856:

> *Her second effort was made in Salem, Mass., at what was known as the Sewall Place Church, and occurred in the following winter. On this occasion she was not entranced till she rose to speak…it seeming to her that a cloud of light enveloped her; so quickly, indeed, did she lose her perception of the scene before her, that when she awoke the impression was firmly fixed in her mind*

> *that she must have fainted. So strong was her belief in this fact, that she asked the chairman of the meeting if it were not so, and was assured by him that the audience had listened, with frequent applause, to a fine lecture of over an hour's duration. She afterwards spoke at the same place several times, with good results, having no further trouble as to her control.*[96]

A brief survey may serve to convey a sense of the variety of activities in Salem or with connections to Salem through the century:

1843 "The Mysterious Lady" at Lyceum Hall

1851, 1857 John R. Patten Jr., 15 Harbor; electropathic, clairvoyant physician

1855 Nathaniel Ingersoll Bowditch; "Gleaner" articles in *Boston Daily Transcript* re: businessman R.G. Shaw, sympathetic to his Spiritualist beliefs and recounting his own experiences in séances [97]

1857 James A. Bassett, 14 or 17 Webb Street; medium

1857 C.C. Jordan, 15 Lafayette; mesmerist ("Mesmeric Examinations"), "Clairvoyant Physician, Magnetizing rooms opposite the Post Office in Bowker Place"

1857 James McGeary, alias Dr. Mack; author, *Healing by Laying-on of Hands* (London, 1879), Salem leather worker who went bankrupt and changed his name, moved to England and became a "mesmeric healer" in 1878; involved in scandals, arrested for larceny, etc. in London

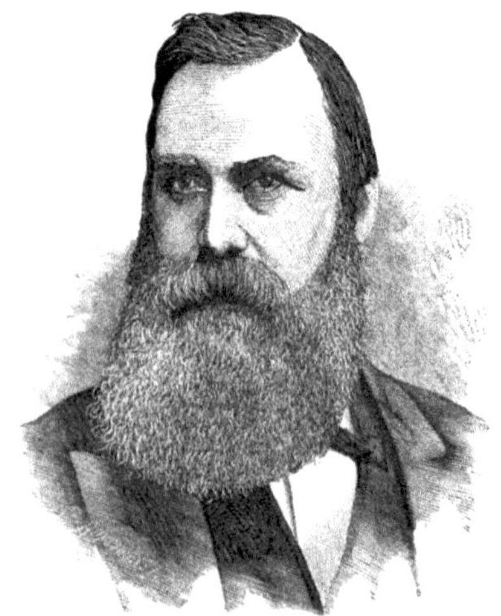

Salem's own "James Mack," former leather worker turned healer.

LYCEUM HALL,

(Church St.) SALEM,

Wednesday Evening, November 12.

"The most strange and bewildering manifestations of some unknown power has ever been introduced to a New York audience."—*N. Y. Herald Sept. 8.*

RELIGIOUS ILLUSTRATED LECTURE

OF

SPIRIT POWER

IN

FULL GAS LIGHT

MISS IDA A. FAY

OF LONDON, ENGLAND.

THE INDESCRIBABLE PHENOMENON!

ENGLAND'S GREATEST

MEDIUM

FOR

PHYSICAL MANIFESTATIONS!

AND

Full Form Materialization.

"Fay—England's Greatest Medium!" A hotly-contested title.

LYCEUM HALL,

(Church St.) SALEM,

Wednesday Evening, November 12

The following Mysterious Manifestations may be expected a each Seance.

Mysterious English

The Most Strange, Unaccountable and Marvellous Phenomena ever presented to the public.

SPIRITUAL PHENOMENON EXPLAINED.

DR. ALBERT MERLIN,

The Inspirational Speaker, will deliver an Illustrated Descriptive

LECTURE

ON THE

Lights and Shadows of Spiritualism.

☞ Do not let religious bigotry detain you from attending, as Spiritualism belongs to all religious creeds. Your religion teaches you that there is a life beyond the grave. Spiritualism demonstrates that such is positively the fact. Convincing proof will be presented to you through the wonderful manifestations of Miss Fay. New and startling manifestations of Spiritual control unheard of previous to the development of this mediumistic marvel. Every manifestation is produced on the *Open Stage* and in

FULL GAS LIGHT!

While a selected committee, chosen by the audience, remains on the stage. Every opportunity will be presented to assist the investigators in their search for Spiritual uths.

EVERYTHING AS ADVERTISED

ou shall see illustrated during the LECTURE by the

2 ENGLISH LADY MEDIUMS. 2

☞ We promise the public that every opportunity will be offered to the skeptical t investigate, and that this will prove to be the finest line of manifestations ever pre sented to an American audience.

A Small Admission Fee will be Charged to defray Expenses

DOORS OPEN AT 7.15. COMMENCING AT 8.

"Lights and Shadows of Spiritualism." "Strange and Unaccountable" indeed.

1858 A.C. Styles, 45 Bond Street; "Independent Clairvoyant," charges sliding scales for "accurate diagnosis"–with or without the patient present

1867 A.C. Robinson; healer

1867 James Rogers Newton (b.1810); healer[98]

1870 Charles H. Foster; famous medium and clairvoyant with international practice

1870 Edward C. Webster (moved to Boston); "Magnetic Physician"

1870 Harry Emerson; gives a "wonderful" cabinet séance at Hubon Hall

1870, 1871 Salem Spiritualist Society, President: Walter Harris; Secretary: Henry M. Robinson (held events at Hubon Hall)

1871 Mrs. E. A. Blair, 166 Bridge Street; "Spirit Artist"

1880 Sophia Cross, 97 Bridge Street; magnetic healer

1880 Irving W. Glidden, son of a tin peddler; magnetic healer

1880 Miss Nellie Everett appears at Mechanic Hall; "wonderful medium," floats in air

1880 Charles H. Harding; clairvoyant

1886 Charles S. "Healer Dennis"; sued and convicted in 1898 for practicing medicine without a license, defended by ex-Senator J.D.H. Gauss of Salem

1886 Lydia M. Buxton, 161 Boston Street; clairvoyant physician, business and test medium

1886 Adeline Barron, 24 Liberty Street; magnetic healer and dyspepsia cure

1891 A.H.Huse, 13 Crombie Street; "Clairvoyant"

1894 First Spiritualist Church, Salem, founded 1894, affiliated with National Spiritualist Association of Churches

1898 Professor J. P. Coffey, "King of Healers," "miracle worker" creates "intense excitement" at the Cadet Armory; magnetic healer

c. 1904 Madam Freeman, 10 Peter Street; "Psychic Palmist and Trance Clairvoyant"

1908 "Willis the Prophet," 6 Elm Street; "Clairvoyant and Palmist"

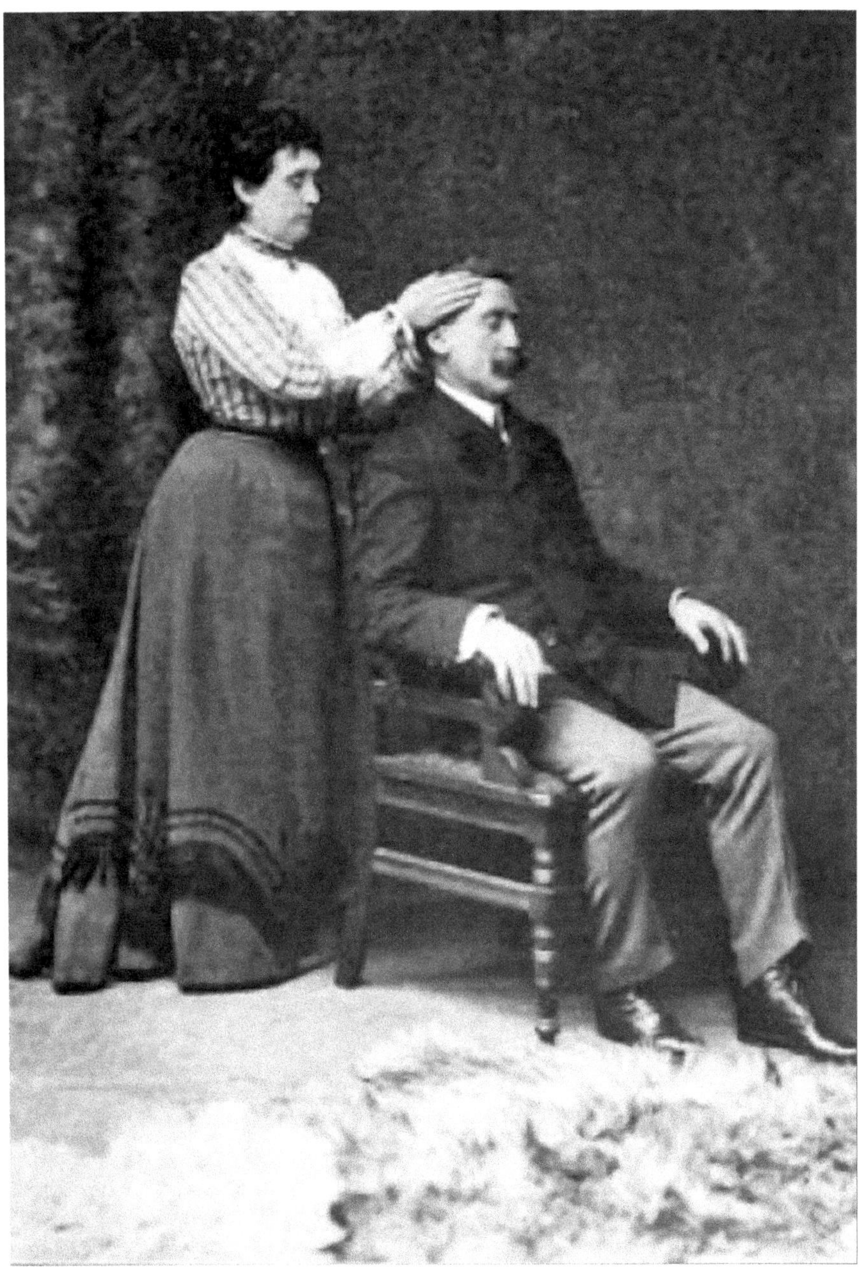

Magnetic healing, a method still in use today.

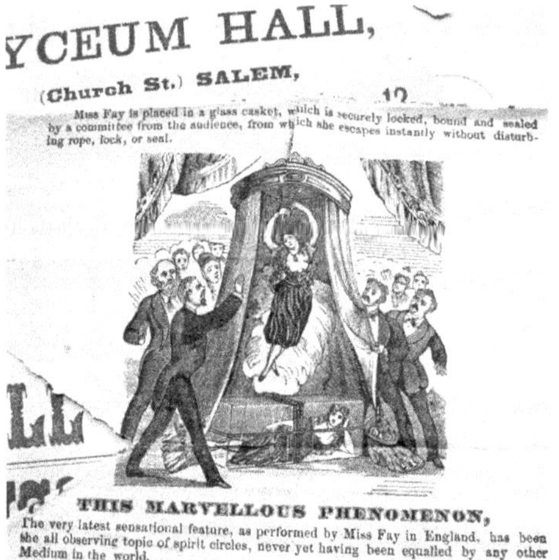

THIS MARVELLOUS PHENOMENON,
The very latest sensational feature, as performed by Miss Fay in England, has been the all observing topic of spirit circles, never yet having been equalled by any other Medium in the world.
Pronounced by the English Press and Public to be the most mysterious Seance ever given.
COMPLETELY BAFFLES ALL SCIENTISTS.
PART SECOND.
MISS MAGGIE HAYDEN
THE MAGNETIC GIRL.
Illustrates the
Psychic or Odic Force
Controlled by her.
1. Introduction of Miss Hayden by her lecturer, Dr. A. Merlin.
2. Miss Hayden *ELECTRIFIES AN UMBRELLA* by her t... thereby forcing strong men about the stage in their efforts to hold it.
3. Miss Hayden, simply touching a cane with the palms of her hands, over... the strongest man.

(Church St.) SALEM,
Wednesday Evening, November 12.
The following Mysterious Manifestations may be expected at each Seance.
The Programme will commence with fastening Miss Fay's feet, hands, and neck ... iron staples with strips of cotton cloth, which are sewn with thread, and further ...ured with court plaster. While in this helpless condition a
SERIES OF BEWILDERING EFFECTS
...l be produced, including Floating Extraordinary, The Mysterious Bell Ringing, The ...riously Knotted Cloth, The Spirit Carpenter, Marvellous Nail and Flying Hammer, ...e Animated Violin, The Circular Hoop and its Extraordinary Power, The Tambourine's Flight, The Working Scissors, The Mouth Organ in its Travels, The Great Goblet and Water Mystery. A puzzle to the scientist; what unseen power produces these results? The Great Fail Sensation.

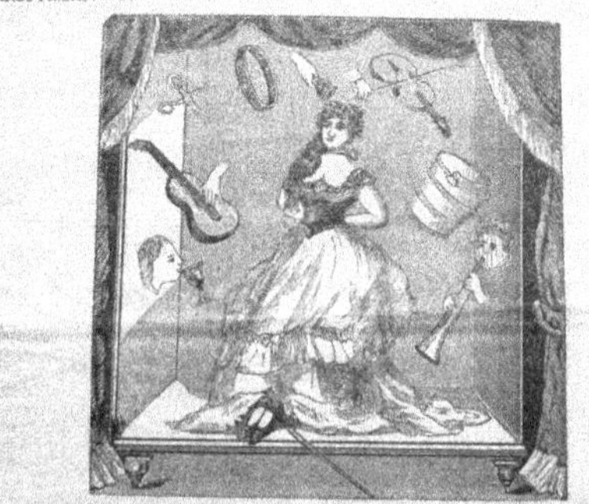

...hile the Medium is in the above condition, *by the aid of some unknown ...ower,*
...N INSTANT CHANGE OF COSTUM...
Will take place.
...omething Never before Accomplished by any Mediu...
AND THE FIRST TIME IN AMERICA.
THE SELF-ACTING KNIFE!
...ich, without any assistance, cuts away the bonds which have secured Miss F... during the Seance.
"The experiment is beyond comprehension."—*Herald*, May, 1882.
THE SPIRITUAL FLIGHT.

"Self-Acting Knife"? "Baffling" isn't the word for it.

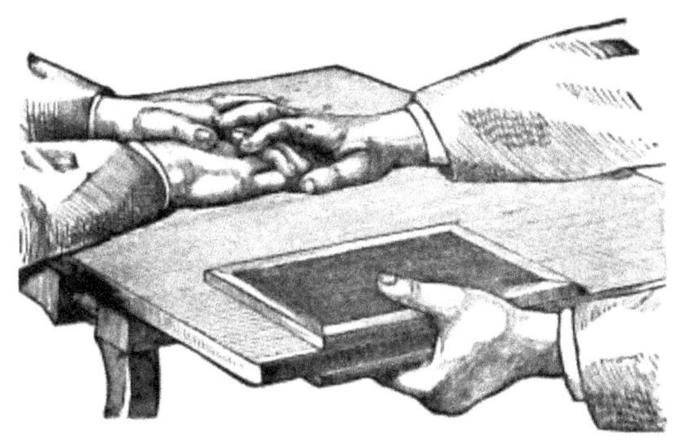

Mediums submitted to a variety of tests to ensure they were not faking. Here, a medium's hands are held by a sitter so that any raps or movements would not be produced by the medium during the sitting.

Temple of the Rosy Cross

Edward H. Brown, Salem attorney, was made Supreme Grand Master of the "Fraternitas Rosæ Crucis for the Western World, Temple of the Rosy Cross; Hierarch of Imperial Eulis" upon the retirement of Freeman Benjamin Dowd from the position, taking office on April 15, 1907. Brown, born in Salem in 1868, and a graduate of the University of New York and Boston University, held the position until his death in 1922. Shy about personal publicity, Brown loved to tinker with machinery, especially engines. This practical side coexisted with his "spiritual-mystical" nature; he was described as "much given to contemplation."

During Brown's tenure Salem was home to an important publishing arm of the Rosicrucians, who incorporate both metaphysics and mysticism in attempts to understand "Divine or Cosmic Consciousness." The Eulian Publishing Company, headed by Brown, was located at 53 Washington Street. It published books by noted members (including Brown's Grand Master predecessor) around the turn of the century. Brown himself wrote only one treatise, *The Sign of Equilibrium*, which was first published in 1917, "just a few years before he was called into the Beyond."[99]

The Last "Salem Witch Trial": 1878

Salem would see yet another "witch trial" in the nineteenth century, and the cause was eerily familiar: religiously sanctioned internecine nastiness.

The Church of Christ, Scientist, founded by Mary Baker Eddy (1821–1910) in 1879, promoted the concept of healing without recourse to medical

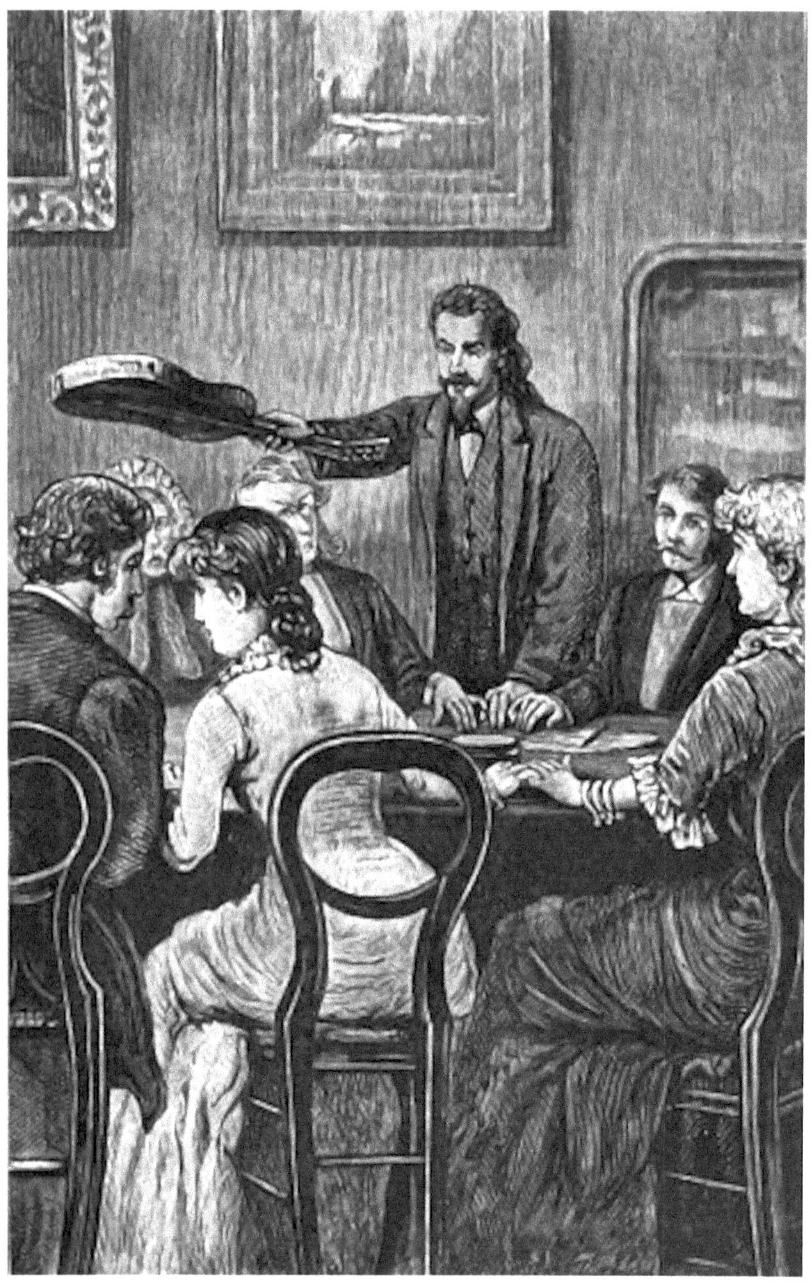

"The medium at work." Exposés and critics abounded as Spiritualistic séances encompassed more and more astounding "effects."

intervention. Meetings of Christian Scientists in Salem "floated" to various venues in Salem, but finally, in 1908, the sect found a home on Lynde Street, in a chapel formerly used by the East Church.[100]

Christian Scientist believer and invalid fifty-year-old Lucretia L.S. Brown, who lived in Ipswich,[101] sought a cure through animal magnetism (something of which Eddy approved). Apparently, at first, the treatment worked, but she relapsed. Brown accused her fellow Christian Scientist, gentle, blue-eyed Daniel Harrison Spofford, a successful "mental healer," of misusing mesmerism to afflict her. Unfortunately, "malicious mesmerism" was also something Eddy believed in, and she was somewhat paranoid about the transference of illness from patient to doctor. So the charge was deemed plausible to Christian Science believers.

Although Spofford had been devoted to Eddy, helping her publish her book *Science and Health with Key to the Scriptures*, she had already severed her ties with him in a fairly nasty way: accusing him of immorality (an action she repeated often with young male disciples). Spofford was charged with witchcraft.

"Having thus prepared her case through the agency of Divine Mind, Mrs. Eddy…went to her lawyer in Lynn and had him draw up a bill of complaint in Miss Brown's name…"[102]

> *Humbly complaining, the Plaintiff, Lucretia L.S. Brown of Ipswich in said County of Essex, showeth unto your Honours, that Daniel H. Spofford, of Newburyport, in said County of Essex, the defendant in the above entitled action, is a mesmerist and practises the art of mesmerism and by his said art and the power of his mind influences and controls the minds and bodies of other persons and uses his said power and art for the purpose of injuring the persons and property and social relations of others and does by said means so injure them.*[103]

The trial was held in Salem Supreme Judicial Court in May 1878. Having helped to set up the trial, Eddy also testified against Spofford. The presiding judge, Horace Gray, dismissed the case three days later. Lucretia Brown appealed; however, the appeal was dismissed in November 1878. Accounts of the trials mention the ridicule that the charge of witchcraft elicited in the more progressive nineteenth century…but one wonders what Salemites said to each other over their dinner tables that spring and winter of 1878.

Afterword

Changing Attitudes

Salem, too, the city of peace, the veritable,
historical spot where the witches were hung,
has a more tolerant generation, at present,
than in the days of Cotton Mather.
—The Medical World: A Journal of Universal Medical Intelligence, *1857*

Though some grumbled about the number of "quacks" in town, and the persistent connection of Salem with witchcraft still mightily troubled many, by the century's end, Salem was fully involved not only with the religion of Spiritualism, but with a variety of occult practices, clairvoyants and mesmeric or magnetic healers of all stripes; attitudes had changed. No longer were witches referred to with "bated breath."

The City of Salem's July 4, 1876 celebrations featured at least two fairly lighthearted references to the witchcraft episode, as evidenced by the printed program. In the Second Division of the immense procession (in which virtually every Salem citizen, group and organization was represented), four cars, filled with thirty-three children, were marshaled by North Church representatives. In the second car, a representation of "The Witch Circle" featured a little girl, dressed as a witch, on a broomstick, "surrounded by little girls roped in with flowers," posed under a verse from Whittier:

Our Witches are no longer old
And wrinkled beldames Satan-sold,
But young and gay and laughing creatures,
With their hearts sunshine on their features.

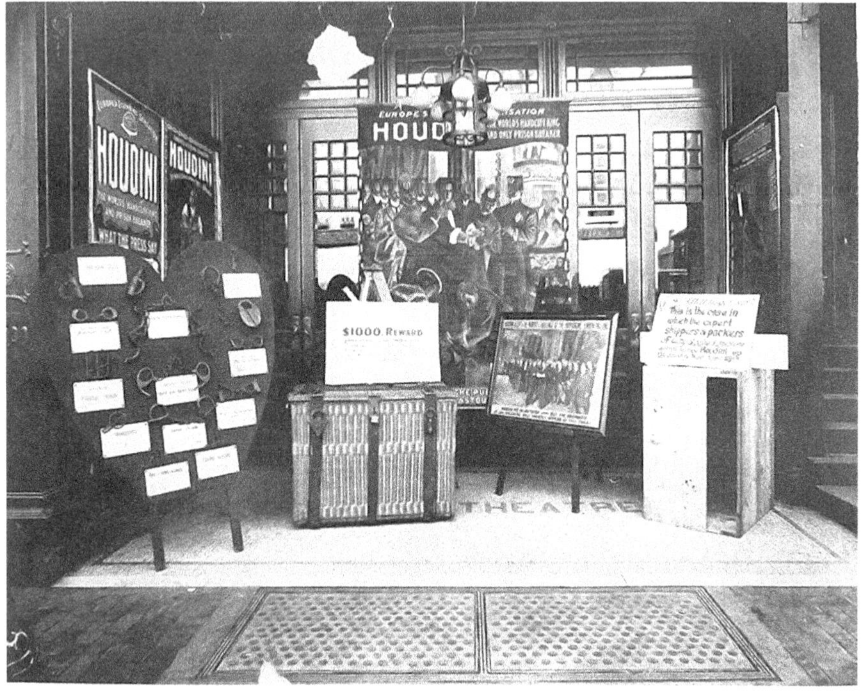

Display in the Salem Theater lobby when Houdini came to town.

The First Universalist Society's section of the procession featured a more sedate exhibit; it is simply described as "No. 12. Salem Witchcraft" and featured "Young Men and women representing an event in local history."

Salem began to exploit some of this more vigorously in a commercial sense. Tourists interested in witchcraft sites, and no longer satisfied with simply seeing the "witch pins" from 1692 (a longstanding tourist thrill, offered at the Court House—eventually discontinued since a number of the pins had disappeared over the years) now found a town supplied with "witchy" souvenir spoons from Daniel Low and Company. All could enjoy lectures on subjects such as Moll Pitcher and her prophecies and could go to numerous entertainments featuring clairvoyants, psychics, magicians, "cabinet miracles" and mind readers—not to mention "miraculous" cure sessions by various healers, often held in auditoriums.

By the end of the century, one could routinely see the image of a witch (usually flying on a broom) used in ads for businesses and civic organizations. Salem offered a "witch" model bicycle, and medals given for winning bicycle

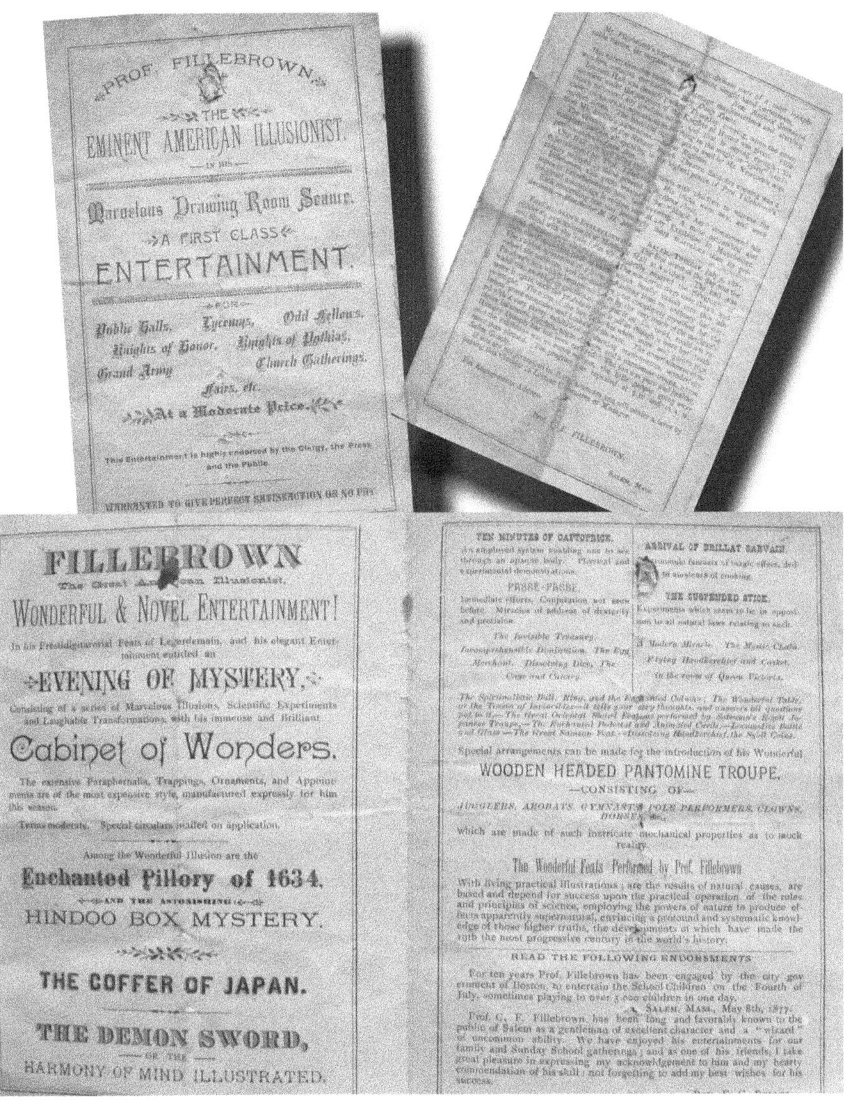

Salem's own famous magician, Charles Fillebrowne—furniture painter turned famous prestidigitator.

races in 1898 used witches in their designs. Grocers used a witch image in newspaper print ads. Postcards with "witch" motifs were available to tourists. More writers tackled "Salem witchcraft," some touting their version in formats we would today call "reader-friendly," "without the tedious detail" of the trials.

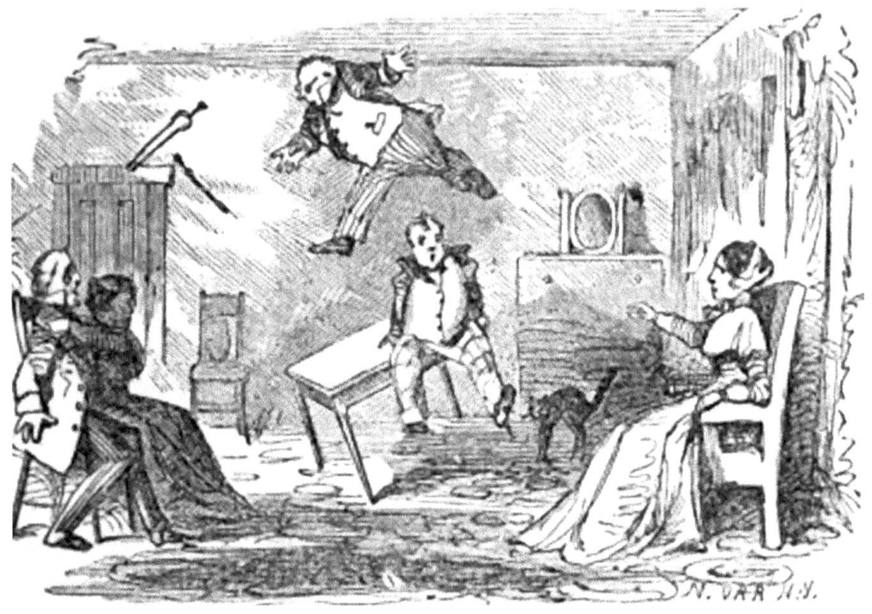

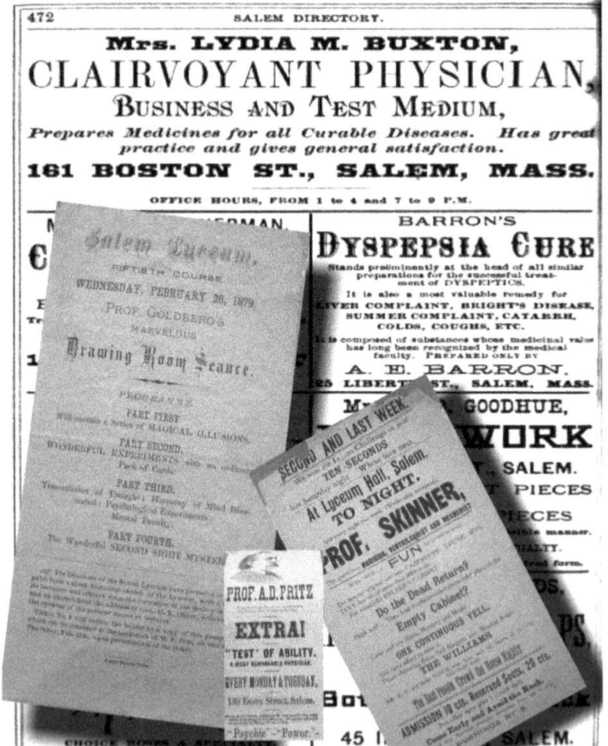

Above: Hiram Mattison was one of the crankiest debunkers of Spiritualism, as this illustration from his book indicates.

Left: Salemites enjoyed a variety of spirit-filled entertainments in the nineteenth century.

The commercialization and trivialization of the "talking board" and planchette tools of serious séances resulted in the famous *Ouija* board; the successful marketing of this toy, produced by Salem's own Parker Brothers, gave an altogether more genial spin to the practice of divination, which some (notably the Rosicrucians) had condemned as dangerous to mental and spiritual health.

Many know that magician, escape artist and anti-Spiritualist investigator Ehrich Weisz, more commonly known as "Harry Houdini" (1874–1926), came to Salem in 1906 and performed shows at the Salem Theater. Houdini (ironically) also engineered a notable escape from a Salem Police Station cell.

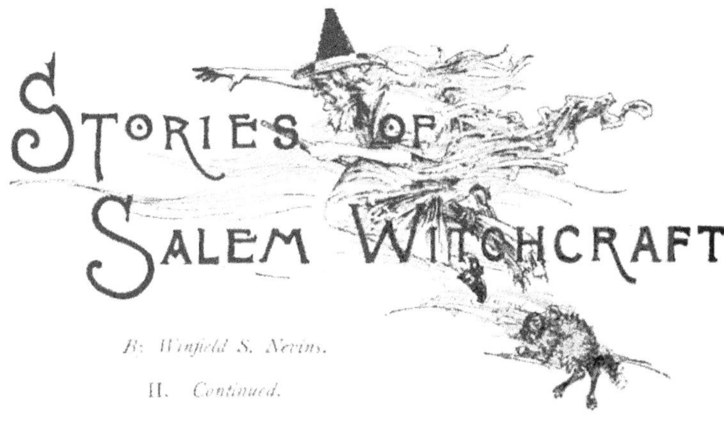

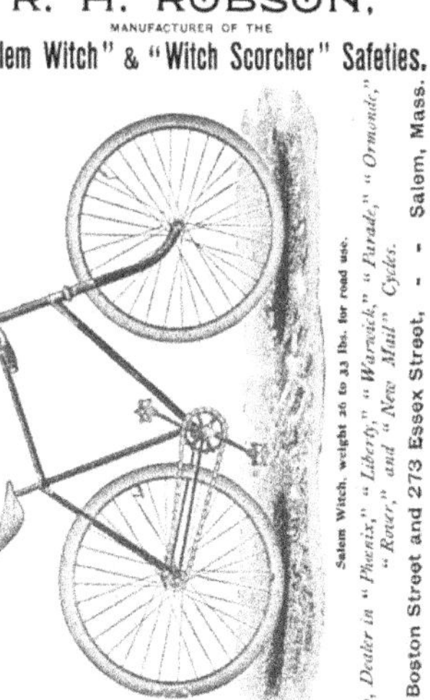

Above: Winfield Scott Nevins (1850–1921) made something of a cottage industry of writing about Salem witchcraft in the last years of the century and until his death.

Right: By the 1890s, the witch design was on souvenir spoons, face cream and grocer's ads (you name it!), and Salem was, commercially at least, reconciled to being "The Witch City."

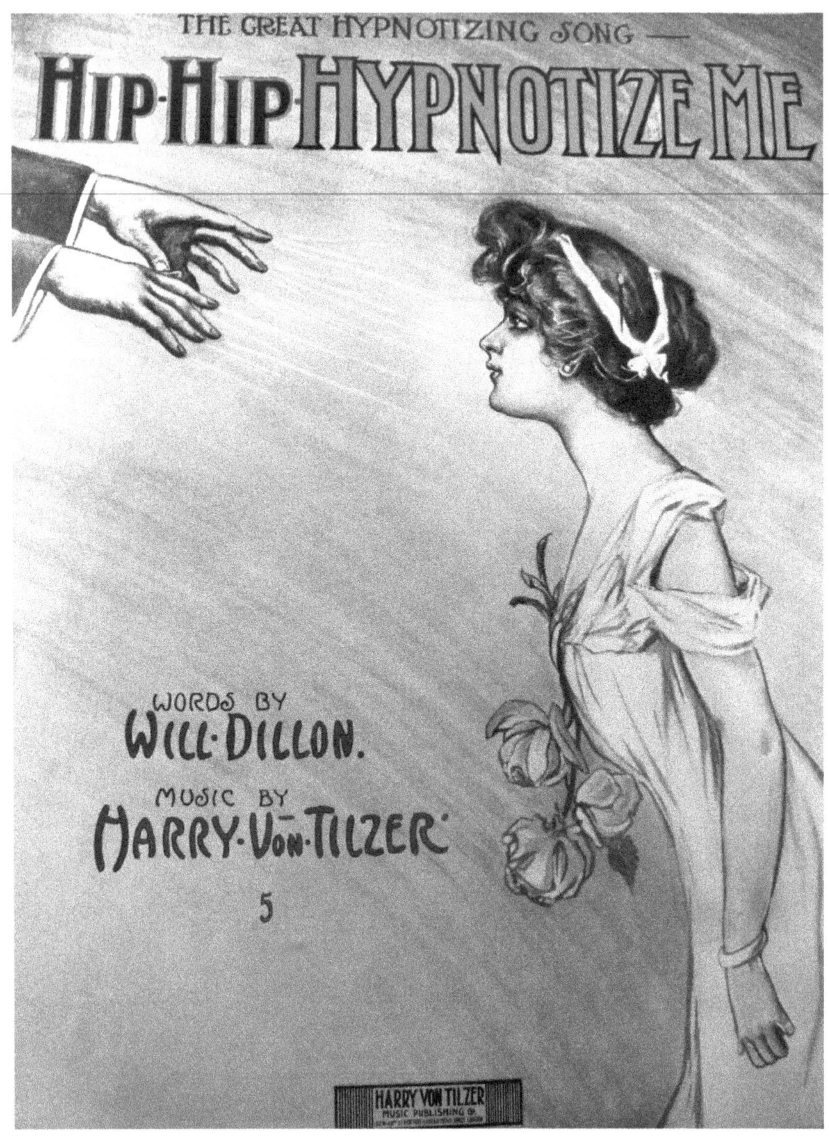

"Hip Hip Hypnotize" us... Mesmerism was part of the culture long after its introduction to America in the early nineteenth century.

Staged "séances" were held in Salem long after his death in 1926. Some of these séances were attended by guests with elaborate engraved invitations in hand. Best characterized as publicity stunts, they attracted media attention to the town, not all of it favorable.

Salem, however, had its own homegrown magician, who, in mid-century, held audiences in thrall and who enjoyed some long-lasting fame, especially in professional (magician) circles.

His name was Charles Francis Fillebrown (b.1834), a former furniture painter, who was, by 1891, known as "America's Oldest Professor of Magic." He was extremely active in mid-century Salem, particularly during the Civil War era, when his shows offered "Magical Mysticism," "Marvelous Illusions" and "Free Prizes" to the audience at Mechanics Hall.

Over a career spanning forty years, he obtained many of his mystifying artifacts, including a "Talking Skull," from "Mr. Chase, of Boston." This prop arrived packed in a large pail, which (the story goes), his wife probably opened, expecting a more prosaic delivery, perhaps a supply of butter—only to see a skull staring at her.[104]

The commercialization of séances, mesmerism and similar activities, always a present danger and temptation to fraud, resulted in a flood of sensationalistic entertainments which exploited gullibility or the hunger for a thrill. Materializations and spirit photography were exposed as humbug, engendering ridicule of Spiritualism, which caused the serious religious intent of most nineteenth-century Spiritualists to recede from popular memory.

Movies and literature, which sensationalized or satirized séances, mediums and the like, added to this degeneration of what had been and still was, for many, a serious spiritual quest.

The work of debunkers from magicians (who saw the Spiritualist phenomenon as the work of rivals) to clergy (ditto) to scientists and from… well, from just plain crabby people…all this served to push the religious intent of Spiritualists even further from general understanding.

Remembrance Revisited

The Oxford English Dictionary defines the etymology of the word "occult" as "classical Latin occultāre to hide, conceal, also in astronomical sense… Of a celestial object: to conceal (an apparently smaller object) from view by passing or being in front."[105]

In its "celestial" sense, the word "occult" gives the distinct impression of a "stage" dominated by a bigger, splashier entity, while something important, unseen or obliquely known, but definitively influential nonetheless, lurks behind the scenes.

Salem, in the nineteenth century, was extremely careful and sensitive about the image it presented to the world. Yet hidden by this dignified celestial projection of an orderly, genteel, utterly rational world loomed an unseen influence on its character and fate.

Salem's 1692 dance with the devil would be cited by those who sought to bolster their critique of "dabbling" in the supernatural…and equally by those who saw in the remarks of scholars about the witchcraft episodes mainstream support for the legitimacy of such occult explorations.

And so the crystal ball rolled on.

Postscript

MARTYRS TO TRUTH" read the headline in the September 13, 1898 Gazette. "Salem's 'Witches' Deserve a Monument...Rev. Dr. Saffords' Sermon On the Outcome of the Awful Delusion."

Saffords's sermon at the Universalist Church (a denomination that counted many Spiritualists among its numbers) attracted a large crowd. His talk ended with a clarion call to celebrate and memorialize the accused witches and celebrate their Christian fortitude in going to ignominious death rather than falsely confess to witchcraft. Rather than lamenting Salem's delusion, rather than blotting it out, as the Essex Institute wished to do, the pastor urged, the city should celebrate its creation of "martyrs to personal integrity."

Charles Upham, too, in his writings on the witchcraft trials, had advocated a monument on Gallows Hill to commemorate the enduring sorrow of Salem in a dignified and righteous way.

Drawings were made and plans drawn up, and many in the nineteenth century were confident that such a monument would be erected directly on the spot where, cruelly, a minister of the gospel had been hanged with his fellow accused innocents, his body thrown haphazardly into a shallow grave as if it were so much rubbish.

No monument or memorial, however, would be erected until another century rolled by from that night in Academy Hall in 1892 when fire danced behind learned men striving to set the record straight on Salem's legacy of supernatural sorrows.

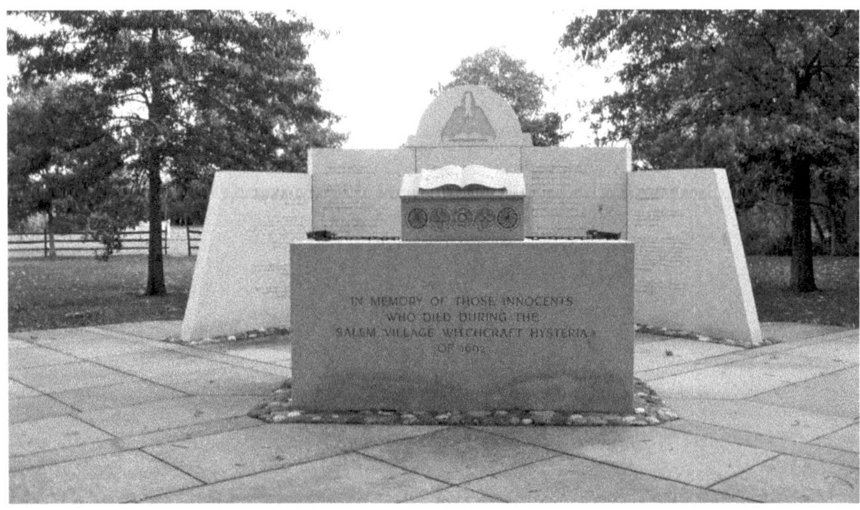

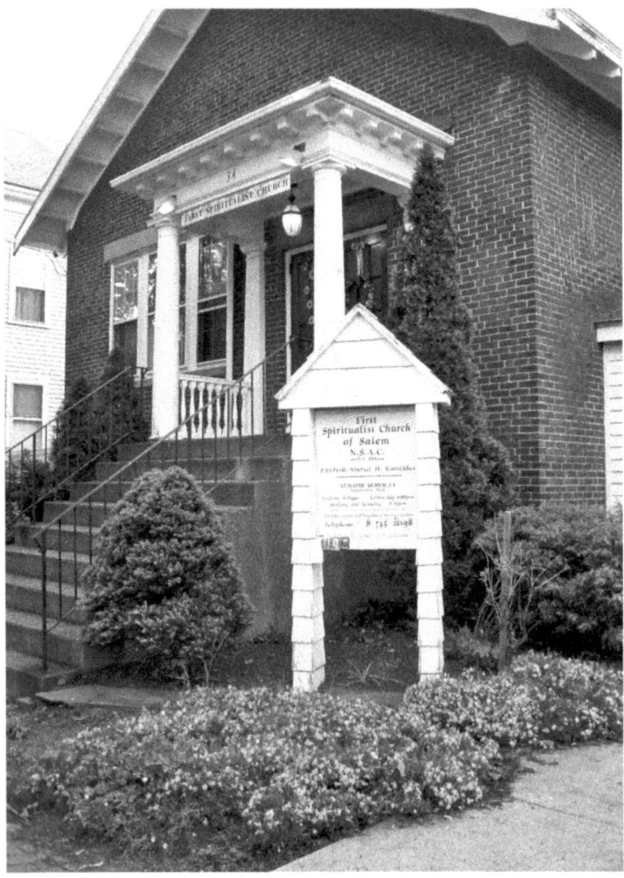

Above: Danvers–a beautiful memorial to the witch trials victims.

Left: First Spiritualist Church, Salem, today.

The modern Salem memorial stands outside Salem's oldest burying point. Each stone is etched with the name of a victim. Their representations, however, endure forever separated from the adjacent sacred ground, forever culled from the main flock as so many sacrificial lambs to humanity's fear of the unknown.

Thus, on Gallows Hill, overlooking and shadowing the city of Salem as it has for centuries, there are no solemn, sacred monuments to horror, death, injustice or sorrow, as nineteenth-century had citizens urged. Instead, the hill harbors a playground, periodically ringing with the regenerating laughter of children as they swing toward the open sky.

Perhaps, in Spiritualist terms, this is just as it should be...signifying the progress of the soul from Calvinist or superstitious darkness to spiritual light, from sorrow to Summerland, from fearful doubt to endless, open horizons.

Notes

Introduction

1. One also sees this, of course, in southern writing, particularly "Old Dominion" (Virginia) writers.

Chapter 1

2. From the hymn "As Shadows Cast by Cloud and Sun," words by Oliver Wendell Holmes (written 1874, published 1877), music by Henry Kemble Oliver (composed 1858, published 1875), (in Christ-Janer, Hughes, & Smith, 1980).
3. M.C.D. Silsbee, *A Half Century in Salem* (Boston and New York: Houghton, Mifflin and Company, 1887), 14.
4. Reverend George Batchelor, in D. Hamilton Hurd, *History of Essex County, Massachusetts: With Biographical Sketches of Many of Its Pioneers and Prominent Men* 1 (Philadelphia: J.W. Lewis & Co., 1888) 16–17.
5. James M. Lindgren, "'That Every Mariner May Possess the History of the World': A Cabinet for the East India Marine Society of Salem," *New England Quarterly* 68, no. 2 (1995), 179–205.
6. Jee Yoon Lee, "'The Rude Contact of Some Actual Circumstance': Hawthorne and Salem's East India Marine Museum," *ELH* 73, no. 4 (Winter 2006), 956.
7. Ibid.
8. Ibid. 955–56.
9. "History of Salem Witchcraft: A Review of Charles W. Upham's Great Work," from the *Edinburgh Review*, with notes by the editor of the *Phrenological Journal*, NY: Fowler & Wells Co., 1886, 8–9. Samuel Roberts Wells (1820–1875) was editor of the *Phrenological Journal*.

10. See the Sarah Orne Jewett Text Project webpage, "JEWETT TO DRESEL: 33 LETTERS By RICHARD CARY," http://www.public.coe.edu/~theller/soj/let/dresel.html.
11. Caroline Howard King and Lousia L. Dresel, *When I Lived in Salem, 1822–1866* (Brattleboro, VT: Stephen Daye Press, 1937), 29–30.
12. John Endicott (also spelled "Endecott") was born circa 1588, most likely in Devon, England, and he died March 15, 1665, in Boston. A truly zealous Puritan, he served as colonial governor of the Massachusetts Bay Colony and is honored as the cofounder of Salem, which, when he arrived, was called "Naumkeag." The traditional story of the renaming of Salem from the native name "Naumkeag" to "Salem" is based on the supposed establishment of good relationships between the original settlers, led by Roger Conant, and the newly arrived governing officials; thus, the town was renamed "Salem" (from the Hebrew word *shalom*, "peace").
13. The publications of the Essex Institute were several, and they have formed, over the years, a fundamentally important resource for any researcher into Salem's history (yet it is woefully difficult to search for particular subjects, since the collection is without a comprehensive, updated, searchable index). Chief among these are the *Historical Collections*, issued as a periodical.
14. Arthur Foote, "A Bostonian Remembers," *Musical Quarterly* 23, no. 1 (1937): 37–44.
15. Patricia Helen Sankus, "Theatrical Entertainments and Other Amusements in Salem, Massachusetts: From the Colonial Period through the Year 1830," PhD thesis, Tufts University, 1981.
16. Charles Stuart Osgood and Henry Morrill Batchelder, *Historical Sketch of Salem, 1626–1879*, Salem: Essex Institute, 1879, 79–101.
17. Jerome Curley, "Then & Now: 16 Lynde St.—From Chapel to Witch Dungeon," *Salem Patch*, June 3, 2012, http://salem.patch.com/articles/from-chapel-to-science-to-witchcraft.
18. Batchelor, *History of Essex County*, 1.
19. Ralph D(elahaye) Paine, *The Ships and Sailors of Old Salem: The Record of a Brilliant Era of American Achievement* (Chicago: A.C. McClurg, 1912), 495.
20. *Salem Gazette*, January 18, 1870, front page.
21. Dr. Neria H. Hebbar, "Swami Vivekananda: The Man and His Mission," http://www.boloji.com/index.cfm?md=Content&sd=Articles&ArticleID=6736. Also see the *Complete Works of Swami Vivekananda* 3, http://www.ramakrishnavivekananda.info/vivekananda/volume_3/vol_3_frame.htm for excerpts of newspaper accounts of his visits to Salem and other places.
22. Mary H. Northend, "Salem of To-day," *New England Magazine* 32 (1905): 95–113.
23. "The Retrospect of the Year," in *Essex Institute Bulletin* XXIV (1892) 156–59.

Chapter 2

24. John S. Haller, *Swedenborg, Mesmer, and the Mind/Body Connection: the Roots of Complementary Medicine* (West Chester, PA: Swedenborg Foundation Press, 2010), 20–21.
25. Ibid., 96.
26. George Trobridge, *Swedenborg: Life and Teaching*, 5th ed. (New York: Swedenborg Foundation, 1992), 137–38.
27. For a biographical sketch of Hargrove, see: "New Church History Fun Facts" at http://newchurchhistory.org/funfacts/?p=170.
28. Hiller is listed as a contributor to the subscription taken for the leveling of the Salem Common in 1801. See *Historical Collections of the Essex Institute* 4, no. 1 (February 1862): 11.
29. American Society for the Dissemination of the Doctrines of the New Jerusalem Church, *New Jerusalem Church Repository for the Years 1817 & 1818* (Philadelphia: Printed and Sold for American Society for the Dissemination of the Doctrines of the New Jerusalem Church by Lydia R. Bailey, No. 10, North Street, 1818), 526.
30. C. Webber, and W.S. Nevins, *Old Naumkeag: An Historical Sketch of the City of Salem, and the Towns of Marblehead, Peabody, Beverly, Danvers, Wenham, Manchester, Topsfield, and Middleton* (Salem, MA: A.A. Smith & Company, 1877), 103.
31. Ibid.
32. Ibid.
33. *History of Essex County* 1, "Cities and Towns," page 61.
34. Educator and all-around intellectual Elizabeth Palmer Peabody (1804–1894) and poet/religious mystic—and "sometimes madman"—Jones Very (1813–1880) also contributed to the rather elusive to define effect of Transcendental ideas in Salem.
35. James Robinson Newhall, *A Lecture on the Occult Sciences: Embracing Some Account of the New England Witchcraft, With an Attempt to Exhibit the Philosophy of Spectre Seeing, Disease Charming, &c. [Published by Request of Auditors]*. Salem: G.W.E & Crafts, 1845.
36. Lewis Edwin Theiss, "Moon and the High Cost of Living," in Smith, A.E., and F. Walton's *New Outlook*, 1916.
37. Since King had not published her memoirs when she died, nor was she necessarily planning to, it is probable that the chapter titles were written by the woman who wrote the preface to the published account, socialite Louisa Loring Dresel (1864–1958), her friend and admirer. Dresel is described as a "connoisseur of the several arts, a lover of books and their makers, a sharp observer and bright glossographer of the passing scene, an inconstant formalist, a deeply confirmed, responsive, amusing companion." Richard Cary, "The Sarah Orne Jewett Project," http://www.public.coe.edu/~theller/soj/let/dresel.html.
38. Caroline Howard King, and Lousia L. Dresel, *When I Lived in Salem, 1822–1866* (Brattleboro, VT: Stephen Daye Press, 1937), 195–99.

39. Joseph Story, *Life and Letters of Joseph Story: Associate Justice of the Supreme Court of the United States*, ed. William W. Story , 2 vols. (London: J. Chapman, 1851), 1:38–39.
40. Mary Ellen Griffin, *Moll Pitcher's Prophecies or the American Sibyl* (Boston: Eastburn Press, 1895), "Introduction."
41. Newhall, *Lecture on the Occult*, 35.
42. See "The Annuals," from the *North American Review* (January 1834): 204. The article discusses a story by Edward Everett in which Moll Pitcher appears ("The Modern Job; or The Philosopher's Stone"). The original story was published in an issue of "The Token and Atlantic Souvenir, A Christmas and New Year's present," a gift annual, for 1834, (pages 269–319). Of interest is the fact that, until 1902, the story, which was published anonymously, was mistakenly attributed to Nathaniel Hawthorne.
43. "Old High Rock" (1847), poetry by Jesse Hutchinson Jr., music by Judson J. Hutchinson.
44. For his account of this gathering, see Andrew Jackson Davis, *Present Age and Inner Life: A Sequel to Spiritual Intercourse. Modern Mysteries Clarified and Explained* (NY: Partridge & Brittan, 1853).
45. Franz Anton Mesmer and George Bloch, *Mesmerism: A Translation of the Original Scientific and Medical Writings of F.A. Mesmer* (Los Altos, CA: W. Kaufman, 1980), xii-xiii.
46. C. Poyen, *Progress of Animal Magnetism in New England: Being a Collection of Experiments, Reports and Certificates, from the Most Respectable Sources: Preceded by a Dissertation on the Proofs of Animal Magnetism* (Boston: Weeks, Jordan & Co., 1837), 198–200.
47. Ibid., 200–201.
48. Robert C. Fuller, *Mesmerism and the American Cure of Souls* (Philadelphia: University of Pennsylvania Press, 1982), 26–27.
49. Osgood and Batchelder, *Historical Sketch of Salem*, 122.
50. Mark C. Carnes, *Secret Ritual and Manhood in Victorian America* (New Haven: Yale University Press, 1989), 28.
51. Ibid., 52
52. F.W. (Frederick William) Evans, *Shakers: Compendium of the Origin, History, Principles, Rules and Regulations, Government, and Doctrines of the United Society of Believers in Christ's Second Appearing* (New York: D. Appleton and Company, 1859).
53. See Catherine L. Albanese, *A Republic of Mind and Spirit: A Cultural History of American Metaphysical Religion* (New Haven: Yale University Press, 2007), 182–83.
54. Ibid., 183–84.
55. William Bentley; Joseph Gilbert Waters; Marguerite Dalrymple; Alice G Waters; Essex Institute. *The Diary of William Bentley, pastor of the East Church, Salem, Massachusetts*, Salem, Essex Institute, 1905–1914, 149.
56. From the 1730s through the 1770s, religious "revitalization" movements spread in the United States. Called the "First Great Awakening," they were also part of a larger movement in England, Scotland and Germany. Evangelical preachers proclaimed a

religion of the heart over the head, biblical revelation over reason. The young, charismatic George Whitefield (1714–1770), who preached to a crowd of six thousand on Salem Common (though far less successfully in Marblehead), was a key leader in this movement.

First Great Awakening preaching featured theatrical thunderings, open weeping and real emotional tour-de-force performances. Advocates of the new understanding ("reborn") were called "New Lights," opponents were "Old Lights" and the movement not only gave birth to the Methodist church but also led to splits in the mainstream Congregationalist and Presbyterian denominations, with resultant political ramifications.

57. William Bentley, et al. *The diary of William Bentley, pastor of the East Church, Salem, Massachusetts*, 154.
58. See Richard L. Bushman and Jed Woodworth, *Joseph Smith: Rough Stone Rolling*, 1st ed. (New York: Alfred A. Knopf, 2005), 14.
59. Lucy Mack Smith, *History of Joseph Smith by His Mother*, 58, as quoted from http://www.gospeldoctrine.com/DoctrineandCovenants/DC%20111.htm. The entire book can be found at Signature Books. The website "Lucy's Book," found at http://signaturebookslibrary.org/?p=9327, contains the Smith biography, comparing each of three published versions side by side.
60. A photo of just such a stone used by Smith, reportedly passed down as an heirloom, is easily found on the web.
61. Quoted from the Joseph Smith Papers, http://josephsmithpapers.org/paperSummary/revelation-6-august-1836-dc-111, Revelation, Salem, MA, 6 Aug. 1836; handwriting of William W. Phelps; in William W. Phelps, Journal, 35–37; CHL, From the website of the Church Historian's Press, Church History Department, the Church of Jesus Christ of Latter-day Saints, Intellectual Reserve, Inc., 2012.
62. Quoted from the official website of the Church of Jesus Christ of Latter-day Saints, "Doctrine and Covenants and Church History Seminary Student Study Guide: Doctrine and Covenants 111—Treasure in Salem," http://seminary.lds.org/manuals/doctrine-and-covenants-and-church-history-seminary-student-study-guide/dc-ssg-4-dc-111.asp. Also see B.H. Roberts, *A Comprehensive History of the Church*, 1:411.
63. Bushman and Woodworth, *Rough Stone Rolling*, 329.
64. For Ashby's account, see the "Book of Abraham Project," http://www.boap.org/LDS/Early-Saints/BAshby.html.
65. Joseph, however, was not a Mormon. According to the *New-England Historical and Genealogical Register Antiquarian Journal* 24, no. 1 (January 1870), he "was ordained as a minister of the Congregational Society at Sharon, Mass., December 19, 1821, and remained there till April 19, 1824. On the 16th of June, following, he was settled at Hamilton, Mass., as successor of Rev. Manasseh Cutler, LL.D., and continued to perform his parochial duties with exemplary punctuality and faithfulness until December 4, 1833, when, owing to ill health, he dissolved his pastoral relation with that church."

66. See "Ancestors of Nathaniel H. Felt," http://www.nhfelt.org/default.asp?PG=doc_NHFChron_Salem. According to the family website, at least one descendant actively participated in occult practices (theosophy) in the 1870s. See the entry on George Henry Felt, http://www.nhfelt.org/default.asp?PG=nhfarchiveancestors.
67. See Michael W. Homer, "Spiritualism and Mormonism: Some Thoughts on Similarities and Differences," in *Dialogue: A Journal of Mormon Thought* 27, no.1, 175.
68. George Edward Ellis, *Memoir of Charles Wentworth Upham* (Cambridge, MA: Press of J. Wilson and Son, 1877), 20.
69. C[harles] W[entworth] Upham, *Lectures on Witchcraft, Comprising a History of the Delusion in Salem, in 1692* (Boston: Carter, Hendee and Babcock, 1831), 41–42.
70. Charles W. Upham, *American Classics: Salem Witchcraft, With an Account of Salem Village and A History of Opinions on Witchcraft and Kindred Subjects* II (NY: Frederick Ungar Publishing Co., Fourth Printing, 1969) [Transcriber's Note: Originally published by Project Gutenberg, 1867.]
71. Robert Grant (1852–1940), Harvard's first PhD in English, wrote of Professor Wendell's character in his memorial article on his colleague. See Robert Grant, "Barrett Wendell (1855–1921)," in *Proceedings of the American Academy of Arts and Sciences* 57, no. 18 (1922): 518–20.

Chapter 3

72. Quotes taken from E.H. Britten and Cairns Collection of American Women Writers, *Modern American Spiritualism: A Twenty Years' Record of the Communion between Earth and the World of Spirits* (self-published, 1870). Also see: Emma Hardinge, *Modern American Spiritualism: A Twenty Years' Record of the Communion between Earth and the World of Spirits* (New Hyde Park, NY: University Books, Inc., 1970), for biographical sketch of Emma Hardinge Britten.
73. According to Worldcat (the Online Computer Library Center, Inc.'s "master catalog," which is, itself, compiled from the catalogs of libraries worldwide), Britten's tour-de-force book was published in twenty-six editions between 1869 and 2000 (in English). It remains a fascinating portrait, not just of Spiritualism, but also of nineteenth-century culture.
74. The term was coined by Horace Greeley in 1852, whose original accounts of the doings of the Fox sisters, published in his *New York Weekly Tribune*, made their séances and mediumship national news; he continued to publish news of "Spiritualists."
75. American Philosophical Society, "'Background Note,' Robert Hare papers, 1764–1858", http://www.amphilsoc.org/mole/view?docId=ead/Mss.B.H22-ead.xml.
76. The First Spiritualist Church still holds circles and meetings in modern Salem in a modest little chapel on Warren Street. It is an affiliate of the National Spiritualist Association of Churches. http://www.firstSpiritualistsalem.org/index.html.
77. Britten, *Modern American Spiritualism*, 9–11.
78. See George C. Bartlett, *The Salem Seer, Reminiscences of Charles H. Foster* (New York: Lovell, Gestefeld & Company, 1891), 45.

79. For a brief introduction to Charles H. Foster, see Maggi Smith-Dalton, *Stories and Shadows from Salem's Past: Naumkeag Notations* (Charleston, SC: The History Press, 2010), 75–77.
80. An inveterate touring musician, Gottschalk gave a successful concert in Salem in June 1862.
81. George C. Bartlett, "Psychic Researches of a Rationalist," *The Humanitarian Review* 9, no. 1 (August 1910): 30.
82. Doyle, *History of Spiritualism*, chapter 2.
83. Allen Putnam, *Spirit works; real but not miraculous: A lecture read at the City Hall in Roxbury, Mass. September 21st. 1853* (Boston: Bela Marsh, 1853), 51–52.
84. Putnam's subsequent wives were Sarah B. Bartlett, 1846, and Frances D. Remick, 1881. He had one child, Abby Hinckley, b. 1833. Not bad for a man who often complained of his poor health.
85. Joseph was the young poet Hawthorne referred to in "The Custom-House," the introduction to *The Scarlet Letter.*
86. A son born to Edward Stanley and Marietta Waters was named Penn Townsend, thus keeping the name alive in the family, as it had been, continuously, since 1651.
87. See Robert S. Rantoul, "Memoir of Henry FitzGilbert Waters," *Proceedings of the Massachusetts Historical Society, Massachusetts Historical Society* 47 (1914), 118–126.
88. It is perhaps interesting to note that Edgar Allen Poe was born at 62 Carver Street.
89. Who this Lydia Webb actually was, or what her relationship was to the Waters family (if any), has been difficult to definitively document as of publication.
90. The Hawthorne children: Una Hawthorne (1844–1877), Julian Hawthorne (1846–1934) and Rose Hawthorne (1851–1926).
91. See *Stories and Shadows from Salem's Past: Naumkeag Notations* for a reproduction of a clipping from the March 28, 1843 *Salem Gazette* advertising a "Mysterious Lady" appearing at Lyceum Hall, which may have been the prototype for the "Veiled Lady" mentioned in the first chapter of Hawthorne's *The Blithedale Romance.*
92. Daniel D. Home's last name was pronounced as "Hume." Hawthorne spelled it the way he heard it.
93. All quotes in this section taken from Nathaniel Hawthorne, *Passages from the French and Italian Note-books of Nathaniel Hawthorne* (Boston: James R. Osgood and Company, 1871), 9–12.
94. Colbert, *Haunted Visions: Spiritualism*, 62.
95. Julian Hawthorne, *Hawthorne Reading: An Essay* (Cleveland, Ohio: The Rowfant Club, 1902), 56–61.

Chapter 4

96. J.W. Day, *Biography of Mrs. J.H. Conant, the World's Medium of the Nineteenth Century: Being a History of Her Mediumship from Childhood to the Present Time: Together with Extracts from the Diary*

of Her Physician; Selections from Letters Received Verifying Spirit Communications Given through Her Organism at the Banner of Light Free Circles; Specimen Messages, Essays, and Invocations from Various Intelligences in the Other Life, Etc., Etc., Etc., Opening Remarks By Allen Putnam, Second Edition (Boston: William White and Company, Banner of Light Office, 1873), 122–23.

97. Nathaniel Ingersoll Bowditch (1805–1861) was the son of Nathaniel Bowditch (1773–1838) and Mary Ingersoll Bowditch (1781–1834); the "Gleaner" articles were otherwise mostly about land grants, genealogy and real estate, which makes the side trip to discussion of séances rather startling.

98. Dr. Newton (b. 1810) was the subject of Alonzo Eliot Newton's *The Modern Bethesda; or, The Gift of Healing Restored. Being some account of the life and labors of Dr. J.R. Newton, healer, with observations on the nature and source of the healing power, and the conditions of its exercise, notes of valuable auxiliary remedies, health maxims, etc.* (New York: Newton, c.1879).

99. Reuben Swinburne Clymer, *The book of Rosicruciae; a condensed history of the Fraternitas Rosaæ Crucis, or Rosy Cross, the men who made the order possible, and those who maintained the fraternity throughout the centuries, together with the fundamental teachings of these men according to the actual records in the archives of the fraternity*, vol. 2 (Quakertown, PA, Philosophical Pub. Co. [1946-49]), 213.

100. See Jerome Curley, "Then & Now: 16 Lynde St.—From Chapel to Witch Dungeon," *Salem Patch*, June 3, 2012, http://salem.patch.com/articles/from-chapel-to-science-to-witchcraft.

101. This witch trial is usually called "The Ipswich Witchcraft Trial" for this reason. However, since the trial took place in Salem, it is also known as the "Second Salem Witch Trial."

102. Georgine Milmine, "Mary Baker G. Eddy," in *McClure's Magazine* 29 (July 1907), 346–47.

103. Georgine Milmine, *The Life of Mary Baker G. Eddy and the History of Christian Science* (New York: Doubleday, Page & Company, 1909), 240–41.

Afterword

104. Hardin J. Burlingame, *Leaves from Conjurers' Scrap Books; or, Modern Magicians and Their Works* (Chicago: Donohue, Henneberry & Co., 1891), 21.

105. *Oxford English Dictionary*, 3rd ed., s.v. "Occult." http://www.oed.com/view/Entry/130167. An entry for this word was first included in *New English Dictionary*, 1902.

Bibliographic Survey

Nothing truly replaces the wondrous on-site archival research I am lucky enough to do at the PEM's Phillips Library (truly my home away from home) or at the Library of Congress.

Yet thanks to the Internet and various organizations including Google, Project Gutenberg, Internet Archive and the wonders of online access to databases of journal articles at my second "homes" of Lesley University and the Boston Conservatory, I've tapped into sources it would have taken me years and a fortune to accumulate for my research. I have been able to access hundreds of digitized nineteenth-century books, magazines, newspapers (including six volumes of the *Banner of Light* in facsimile) and all kinds of primary source ephemera and illustrations online.

The listing of all the resources I consulted would make another book on its own, so for now, I'll merely highlight *some* of the secondary (book) resources I found useful as I sought to provide frameworks for the hundreds of primary materials I consulted. This is a very small, selective list adding to those titles you'll find in the endnotes.

Occult

Bown, Nicola, Carolyn Burdett, and Pamela Thurschwell. *The Victorian Supernatural.* (Cambridge, UK: Cambridge University Press, 2004).

Gutierrez, Cathy. *The Occult in Nineteenth-Century America.* (Aurora, CO: Davies Group, 2005).

Melechi, Antonio. *Servants of the Supernatural: The Night Side of the Victorian Mind.* (London: Arrow, 2009).

Personalities

Coale, Samuel. *Mesmerism and Hawthorne: Mediums of American Romance.* (Tuscaloosa: University of Alabama Press, 1998).

Colbert, Charles. *Haunted Visions: Spiritualism and American Art.* (Philadelphia: University of Pennsylvania Press, 2011).

Hawthorne, Nathaniel, Seymour Gross Lee, and Rosalie Murphy. *The Blithedale Romance: An Authoritative Text, Backgrounds and Sources, Criticism.* (New York: Norton, 1978).

Marshall, Megan. *The Peabody Sisters: Three Women Who Ignited American Romanticism.* (Boston: Houghton Mifflin, 2005).

Mellow, James R. *Nathaniel Hawthorne in His Times.* (Boston: Houghton Mifflin, 1982).

Moore, Margaret B. *The Salem World of Nathaniel Hawthorne.* (Columbia: University of Missouri Press, 1998).

Religion in America

Ahlstrom, Sydney E. *A Religious History of the American People.* (New Haven, CT: Yale University Press, 1972).

Albanese, Catherine L. *Nature Religion in America: From the Algonkian Indians to the New Age.* (Chicago: University of Chicago Press, 1991).

Salem and United States History

Adams, Gretchen A. *The Specter of Salem: Remembering the Witch Trials in Nineteenth-Century America.* (Chicago: University of Chicago Press, 2010).

DeRosa, Robin. *The Making of Salem: The Witch Trials in History, Fiction and Tourism.* (Jefferson, NC: McFarland, 2009).

Morrison, Dane Anthony, and Nancy Schultz Lusignan. *Salem: Place, Myth, and Memory.* (Boston: Northeastern University Press, 2004).

Schantz, Mark S. *Awaiting the Heavenly Country: The Civil War and America's Culture of Death.* (Ithaca, NY: Cornell University Press, 2008).

Scientific Explorations and Mesmerism

Blum, Deborah. *Ghost Hunters: William James and the Search for Scientific Proof of Life after Death.* (New York: Penguin Press, 2006).

Fuller, Robert C. *Mesmerism and the American Cure of Souls.* (Philadelphia: University of Pennsylvania Press, 1982).

Secret Societies and Esoteric Elements

Beresniak, Daniel. *Symbols of Freemasonry.* (New York: Barnes & Noble Books, 2003).

Spiritualism

Birnes, William J., and Joel Martin. *The Haunting of America: From the Salem Witch Trials to Harry Houdini.* (New York: Forge, 2009).

Braude, Ann. *Radical Spirits: Spiritualism and Women's Rights in Nineteenth-Century America.* (Bloomington: Indiana University Press, 2001).

Buescher, John B. *The Other Side of Salvation: Spiritualism and the Nineteenth-Century Religious Experience.* (Boston: Skinner House Books, 2004).

Carroll, Bret E. *Spiritualism in Antebellum America.* (Bloomington: Indiana University Press, 1997).

Doyle, Arthur Conan. *The History of Spiritualism.* (Newcastle, England: Classic Scholars Publishing Classic Texts, 2009).

Owen, Alex. *The Darkened Room: Women, Power, and Spiritualism in Late Victorian England.* (Philadelphia: University of Pennsylvania Press, 1990).

I also consulted books on Nathaniel Hawthorne written by his son, Julian, and his daughter Rose.

Image Credits

Prologue

Page 20. (Left) From John Ireland and John Nichols, FSA, "Credulity, Superstition, and Fanaticism" (1760) from *Hogarth's Works: with Life and Anecdotal Descriptions of his Pictures.* Second Series (Edinburgh: Oliphant, Anderson, & Ferrier, 1883).

(Right) "Trial of George Jacobs of Salem for Witchcraft" from a painting by Tompkins Harrison Matteson 1855, still hanging in the foyer of the Essex Institute (now the Phillips Library of the Peabody Essex Museum). Photographed by the Detroit Publishing Company, courtesy of the Library of Congress.

Page 21. Photo by Maggi Smith-Dalton.

Page 22. (Right) From Daniel P. Toomey, *Massachusetts of Today: A memorial of the state, historical and biographical, issued for the World's Columbian Exposition at Chicago* (Boston: Massachusetts Board of Managers, Columbia Publishing Company, 1892).

(Bottom) From William Cullen Bryant, ed., *Picturesque America, or, The land we live in. A delineation by pen and pencil of the mountains, rivers, lakes, water-falls, shores, cañons, valleys, cities, and other picturesque features of our country—Revised edition* (NY: D. Appleton and Company, 1894).

Chapter 1

Page 27. From *Frank Leslie's Illustrated Newspaper*, September 1869.

Page 42. (Left) Kate Tannatt Woods, from Frances E. Willard; Mary A[shton] [Rice] Livermore (Eds.), *A Woman of the Century: fourteen hundred-seventy biographical sketches accompanied by portraits of leading American women in all walks of life* (Buffalo, NY: Charles Wells Moulton, 1893).

(Right) Swami Vivekananda from Lewis Pyle Mercer, *Review of the world's religious congresses of the World's congress auxiliary of the World's Columbian exposition, Chicago, 1893* (Chicago and New York, Rand, McNally & Co., 1893).

Page 44. "Trial exhibition of Bell's telephone for the transmission of sound by electricity, operated between Salem & Boston, Mass., Mar. 15 ... Bell addressing a party of scientific men. Wood engraving in Frank Leslie's Illustrated Newspaper, Mar. 31, 1877, after E. R. Morse." Library of Congress, LOC Reproduction number: LC-USZ62-794.

Chapter 2

Page 49. From William White, *Swedenborg: His Life and Writings,* (London: William White, 1856).

Page 52. From Winfield S. Nevins, *Witchcraft in Salem Village in 1692: Together with Some Account of Other Witchcraft Prosecutions in New England and Elsewhere* (Salem, MA: North Shore Publishing Company; Boston: Lee and Shepard, 1892).

Page 55. From Samuel Adams Drake, *Our Colonial Homes* (Boston: Lee and Shepard, 1894).

Page 58. From Ellen M. Griffin, *Moll Pitcher's Prophecies: or, The American Sibyl* (Boston: Eastburn Press, 1895). Private collection of author.

Page 60. From C[harles] F[erson] Durant, *Pliny Merrick, Exposition, or A new theory of animal magnetism: with a key to the mysteries: demonstrated by experiments with the most celebrated somnambulists in America: also, strictures on "Col. Wm. L. Stone's letter to Doct. A. Brigham"*, (New York: Wiley & Putnam, 1837).

Page 62. Illustration from John R. Musick; F.A. Carter *The Witch of Salem; or Credulity Run Mad* Project Gutenberg, 26282, (2008) (transcribed from the book by John Roy Musick, originally published New York [etc.] Funk & Wagnalls Co., 1893).

Page 64. From Andrew Jackson Davis, *The Magic Staff: An Autobiography of Andrew Jackson Davis* (New York: J.S. Brown & Co., Boston: Bela Marsh, 1837).

Page 67. Photo by Maggi Smith-Dalton.

Page 68. From Lauron William De Laurence, *Hypnotism a complete system of method, application and use, including all that is known in the art and practice of mesmerism and mental healing, prepared for the self-instruction of beginners as well as for the use of advanced students and practitioners* (Chicago & New York, Henneberry Co., 1900).

Page 77. From Joseph Fielding Smith, *Essentials in Church History* (Salt Lake City, Utah: The Church of Jesus Christ of Latter-day Saints, 1922).

Page 79. Photo by Maggi Smith-Dalton.

Page 81. From Nevins, *Witchcraft in Salem Village*, 1892.

Page 83. From George Edward Ellis, *Memoir of Charles Wentworth Upham.* Reprinted from the Proceedings of the Massachusetts Historical Society, December 1876 (Cambridge, MA: Press of John Wilson and Son, 1877).

Page 86. From Lewis Edwards Gates, Barrett Wendell and Horace Elisha Scudder, *Studies in American Literary Life* (Philadelphia: Booklovers Library, 1901).

Chapter 3

Page 90. From Emma Hardinge [Britten], *Modern American Spiritualism: A Twenty Years' Record of the Communion Between Earth and the World of Spirits*, Second Edition (New York: The Author/ New York Publishing Company, 1870).

Page 91. From Robert Hare, *Experimental investigation of the spirit manifestations: demonstrating the existence of spirits and their communion with mortals: doctrine of the spirit world respecting heaven, hell, morality, and God. Also, the influence of Scripture on the morals of Christians* (New York: Partridge & Brittan, 1855).

Page 93. Banner of Light advertisement from Facts, (Boston: Facts Publishing Company, Vol. 1, Nos. 1 & 2, [March and June] 1882); Masthead banner from an issue of The Banner of Light. Many thanks to the editors of the online archives of The International Association of Spiritualist and Occult Periodicals (IAPSOP), which provided several runs of *Banner of Light* online. http://www.iapsop.com/archive/materials/banner_of_light/

Page 94. Wikipedia. Attributed Source for image on Wikipedia: Joseph Glanvill, *Saducismus Triumphatus* (First Edition, London: 1681).

Page 96. From *Confessions of a Medium [By Chapman]* (London: Griffith & Farran; NY: E.P. Dutton & Co., 1882).

Page 98. From Hiram Mattison (1811–1868) (probably; he seems to be the most likely candidate for the anonymous author of this book, writing under the name "Searcher after truth"), *The rappers, or, The mysteries, fallacies, and absurdities of spirit-rapping, table-tipping, and entrancement* (New York: H. Long & Brother, 1854).

Page 101. From Ernest Abraham Hart, *Hypnotism, Mesmerism and the New Witchcraft* (New York: D. Appleton and Co., 1896).

Page 102. From Thomas Olman Todd, *Hydesville: The Story of the Rochester Knockings, Which Proclaimed the Advent of Modern Spiritualism* (Sunderland, England: Keystone Press, 1905).

Page 105. Courtesy Phillips Library, Peabody Essex Museum, Salem, Massachusetts.

Page 107. From Davis, *The Magic Staff*, 1837.

Page108. From Andrew Jackson Davis, *The Great Harmonia: A Philosophical Revelation of the Natural, Spiritual, and Celestial Universe (The Teacher)* 2 (Rochester, NY: The Austin Publishing Co., 1910).

Page 110. From Davis, *The Magic Staff*, 1837.

Page 111. Photo by Maggi Smith-Dalton.

Page 112. From Caroline Ticknor, *Hawthorne and his Publisher*, (Boston: Houghton Mifflin, 1913).

Page 115. (Top) From Ticknor, *Hawthorne and his Publisher*, 1913.

(Bottom) From Henry James, *William Wetmore Story and his friends; from letters, diaries, and recollections* (Boston: Houghton, Mifflin & Co., 1903).

Chapter 4

Page 118. From James Mack, *Healing by Laying-on of Hands* (London: J.Burns,1879).

Page 119. Courtesy Phillips Library, Peabody Essex Museum, Salem, Massachusetts.

Page 121. From De Laurence, *Hypnotism: A Complete System of Method*, 1900.

Page 122. Courtesy Phillips Library, Peabody Essex Museum, Salem, Massachusetts.

Page 123. From *Facts,* March and June, 1882.

Page 124. From Confessions of a Medium, 1882.

Afterword

Page 128. Courtesy collection of Nelson Dionne.

Page 129. Courtesy Phillips Library, Peabody Essex Museum, Salem, Massachusetts.

Page 130. (Top) From Hiram Mattison, *Spirit Rapping Unveiled! An exposé of the origin, history, theology and philosophy of certain alleged communications from the spirit world, by means of "spirit rapping," "medium writing, " "physical demonstrations, " etc.* (NY: J.C. Derby, 1855).

(Left) Ads from nineteenth-century Salem city directories; broadsides and ephemera. Courtesy Phillips Library, Peabody Essex Museum, Salem, Massachusetts.

Page 131. (Top) From Salem Firemen's Relief Association, List of fire alarm boxes, street directory and book of general information, 1892 : also, fire alarm calls of Lynn, Peabody and Beverly, with cuts of theatre plans of Salem and Boston (Salem: F.J. Flanigan, 1892).

(Right) From *The New England Magazine: An Illustrated Monthly* 6, 1892.

Page 132. "Hip Hip Hypnotize," words: Will Dillon, music: Harry Von Tilzer (New York: Harry Von Tilzer Music Publishing Co., 1910). Photo by Maggi Smith-Dalton; sheet music in the private collection of author.

Postscript

Page 136. Photos by Maggi Smith-Dalton.

Index

N

O

P

Q

R

S

T

U

V

W

Y

About the Author

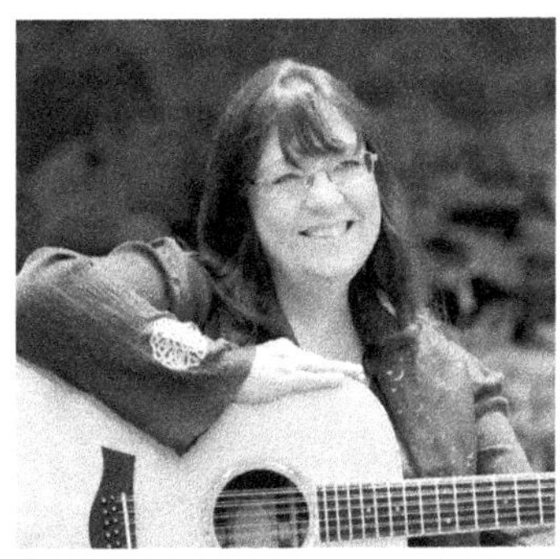

Photograph by Daniel St. John, Lightshed Photography, Salem, Massachusetts.

Maggi Smith-Dalton began her singing career in cabarets and nightclubs and has maintained a parallel career as a historian most of her life. With her husband, Jim, she tours nationwide as a concert artist. She has performed as a soloist with large domestic and international choirs, recorded five albums to date and hosted an NPR public radio station classical music show.

Maggi is a prizewinning short story writer and has a long history of writing feature articles and columns for magazines and newspapers. In 2010, she began to write a weekly history column for the *Boston Globe* (boston.com).

She holds a master's degree in American Studies, and her current scholarly work focuses on historic civic rituals that incorporate music as a primary element, a subject on which she has presented domestically and abroad. Her first book of Salem history, *Stories and Shadows From Salem's Past*, was published by The History Press in 2010.

Maggi is usually running like the White Queen as president of the Institute for Music, History and Cultural Traditions, which runs two public programs: the American History and Music Project and the Salem History Society. In 2010, she was elected to the council of the New England American Studies Association.

She loves to garden and usually can be found muttering to herself as she happily rakes, plants, feeds and waters various living things, including herself. The squirrels, it is rumored, are used to her soliloquies by now, although one wonders what the neighbors think.

www.ingramcontent.com/pod-product-compliance
Lightning Source LLC
LaVergne TN
LVHW052341100826
845147LV00021B/1138

* 9 7 8 1 6 0 9 4 9 5 5 1 0 *